LEVEL ONE

Sound Advice
Theory and Ear Training

Brenda Braaten and **Crystal Wiksyk**

Series Editor
Laura Beauchamp-Williamson

Illustrations by Paul McCusker

© Copyright 2006 The Frederick Harris Music Co., Limited
All Rights Reserved

ISBN 978-1-55440-031-7

Design & Production: First Image
Music Typesetter: Ken Gee

Library and Archives Canada Cataloguing in Publication

Braaten, Brenda, 1952-
Sound advice : theory and ear training / Brenda Braaten and
Crystal Wiksyk ; illustrations by Paul McCusker.

Accompanied by audio tracks, available online.
To be complete in 8 vol.
Complete contents: Level 1 – Level 2 – Level 3 – Level 4 –
   Level 5– Level 6 – Level 7 – Level 8.
ISBN 1-55440-031-7 (v. 1).–ISBN 1-55440-032-5 (v. 2).–
ISBN 1-55440-033-3 (v. 3).–ISBN 1-55440-034-1 (v. 4).–
ISBN 1-55440-035-X (v. 5).–ISBN 1-55440-036-8 (v. 6).–
ISBN 1-55440-037-6 (v. 7).–ISBN 1-55440-038-4 (v. 8)

1. Music theory. 2. Ear training. I. Wiksyk, Crystal, 1959-
II. McCusker, Paul III. Title.

MT7.B794S72 2006   781   C2005-907128-1

Contents

Preface for Teachers 6

How to Use This Book 7
Lesson Organization
Completing the Ear-Training Worksheets
Charts and Games
Suggestions for Daily Ear-Training Practice

Lesson 1

Learning Guide 10
  Beat and Tempo
  Notes
  Duration: Quarter Notes and Half Notes
  The Quarter Note ♩
  The Half Note ♩
  Rhythm Jumble
Theory Worksheet 12
Ear-Training Worksheet 13

Lesson 2

Learning Guide 14
  Pitch
  Staff
  Line Notes
  Space Notes
  Stem Direction
Theory Worksheet 16
Ear-Training Worksheet 17

Lesson 3

Learning Guide 18
  Rhythmic Dictation
Theory Worksheet 19
Ear-Training Worksheet 20

Lesson 4

Learning Guide 21
  The Music Alphabet
  The Keyboard
  The Treble Clef and Treble Staff
  How to Draw a Treble Clef
  Ledger Lines
  Treble-Staff Landmarks
Theory Worksheet 24
Ear-Training Worksheet 26

Lesson 5

Learning Guide 27
  The Bass Clef and Bass Staff
  How to Draw a Bass Clef
  Bass-Staff Landmarks
  A Closer Look at Middle C
Theory Worksheet 29
Ear-Training Worksheet 31

Lesson 6

Learning Guide 32
  The Grand Staff
  Middle C on the Grand Staff
Theory Worksheet 33
Ear-Training Worksheet 34

Lesson 7

Learning Guide 35
  Naming Notes on the Grand Staff
  Mad Music
Theory Worksheet 36
Ear-Training Worksheet 37

Lesson 8

Learning Guide 38
  The Eighth Note ♪
  Rhythm Jumble
  Rhythmic Dictation with Eighth Notes
  A Closer Look at Stem Direction
Theory Worksheet 41
Ear-Training Worksheet 42

Lesson 9

Learning Guide 43
  Scales
  Singing the C Major Scale, Ascending
  Intervals
  2nds (Steps)
Theory Worksheet 45
Ear-Training Worksheet 46

Lesson 10

Learning Guide 47
  3rds (Skips)
  Singing the C Major Scale, Ascending
    and Descending
Theory Worksheet 48
Ear-Training Worksheet 49

Lesson 11

Learning Guide 50
  Bar Lines and Measures
  Meter
  Duple Meter
  Time Signature 2/4
  Measure Numbers
Theory Worksheet 52
Ear-Training Worksheet 53

Lesson 12

Learning Guide 54
  Ties
  New Rhythmic Unit ♩♪
  Rhythm Jumble Games
Theory Worksheet 56
Ear-Training Worksheet 57

Lesson 13

Learning Guide 58
  The Quarter Rest 𝄽
  How to Draw a Quarter Rest
  Naming Intervals
  The Sound of Major 2nds and Major 3rds
Theory Worksheet 60
Ear-Training Worksheet 61

Lesson 14

Learning Guide 62
  5ths
  Perfect Intervals
  The Sound of the Perfect 5th
Theory Worksheet 64
Ear-Training Worksheet 65

Lesson 15

Learning Guide 66
  The Dotted Half Note ♩.
  Triple Meter
  New Time Signature 3/4
Theory Worksheet 67
Ear-Training Worksheet 68

Lesson 16

Learning Guide 69
  4ths
  The Sound of the Perfect 4th
  Interval Singing Drill
Theory Worksheet 71
Ear-Training Worksheet 72

Lesson 17

Learning Guide 73
  Half Steps
  White-Key Half Steps
  Accidentals: The Sharp Sign ♯
  How to Draw a Sharp Sign
Theory Worksheet 76
Ear-Training Worksheet 77

Lesson 18

Learning Guide 78
  Accidentals: The Flat Sign ♭
  How to Draw a Flat Sign
Theory Worksheet 79
Ear-Training Worksheet 80

Lesson 19

Learning Guide 81
  Whole Steps
  Major and Minor 2nds
  The Sound of the Minor 2nd
Theory Worksheet 84
Ear-Training Worksheet 86

Lesson 20

Learning Guide 87
  Whole Steps and Half Steps in
    the Major Scale
  The C Major Scale
  The G Major Scale
  The F Major Scale
Theory Worksheet 88
Ear-Training Worksheet 89

Lesson 21

Learning Guide 90
  Facts about Accidentals
  Accidentals: The Natural Sign ♮
  How to Draw a Natural Sign
  Octaves (8ves)
  The Sound of the Perfect 8ve
Theory Worksheet 92
Ear-Training Worksheet 93

Lesson 22

Learning Guide 94
  Quadruple Meter
  New Time Signature 4/4
  The Whole Note o
  The Whole Rest
  The Half Rest
Theory Worksheet 96
Ear-Training Worksheet 98

Lesson 23

Learning Guide 99
  Key Signatures
Theory Worksheet 100
Ear-Training Worksheet 101

Lesson 24

Learning Guide 102
  Terms and Symbols
  Legato
  Slur
  Staccato
Theory Worksheet 104
Ear-Training Worksheet 105

Theory Examination 106

Melody Master 109

Charts and Games

Note-Value Comparison Chart 113
Drawing Symbols Chart 114
Rhythm Jumble Chart 115
Rhythm Jumble Games 116
Song Clue Chart 117
Mad Music Game 118

Answer Keys

Ear Training 122
Melody Master 146
Mad Music 149

Appendix

Sight-Singing Syllable Systems 152

Preface for Teachers

Too often, music theory instruction emphasizes written concepts, with little or no attention paid to the way things actually *sound*. Our teaching philosophy is simple: never take the *sound* out of music theory instruction!

The *Sound Advice* program relates musical sounds to their symbols by combining written and aural theory. Throughout the series, theoretical concepts are introduced in a clear, concise manner and immediately reinforced with written worksheets and ear-training assignments. Later volumes also provide students with lessons on musical style and an introduction to composition.

Students of all instruments, including those who study voice, can use *Sound Advice*. Ideally, the program should be started under the guidance of a teacher as early as possible in a student's musical training. *Sound Advice* can be used successfully in private lessons, small group sessions, or in classroom teaching. On average, most private students will complete one lesson per week, while students in semester-long theory or musicianship classes may progress at a faster pace. Either way, the lesson planning is taken care of for teachers. Each lesson is carefully organized so that students are presented with an appropriate amount of new material while continuing to review previously introduced concepts. Constant review is an important feature of *Sound Advice*.

Each *Sound Advice* lesson consists of a Learning Guide that introduces new material, a written Theory Worksheet, and an Ear-Training Worksheet to be completed using the accompanying recordings. There are also a number of Charts and Games that reinforce material learned in the lessons.

Ear-training activities in Level 1 include sight singing of melodies and rhythms, rhythm singbacks and clapbacks, melody playbacks and singbacks, identification of intervals, editing (error detection), rhythmic dictation, and melodic dictation. Answers to all of the ear-training activities in *Sound Advice* can be checked by the student. We have provided Ear-Training Answer Keys so that students can mark their work at home immediately after completing each exercise. Teachers can easily monitor their ear-training progress by viewing the marked pages at the next lesson, and ear-training exercises can be repeated as many times as necessary for extra practice. Written Theory Worksheets are to be marked by the teacher.

It is important that teachers and students, as well as parents, understand the *How to Use This Book* section (pp. 7–9). For younger students, the teacher's guidance may be needed to get them started.

While *Sound Advice* can be used to prepare students for the ear-training and theory components of several major examining boards,[1] our main goal is to help *all* students become musically literate—to have a better understanding of how music "works" and to continue to develop a deeper appreciation for music throughout their lives.

Brenda Braaten and *Crystal Wiksyk*

---

[1] Level 1 covers ear-training requirements for The Royal Conservatory of Music (RCM) Grade 1 piano examinations, Victoria Conservatory of Music (VCM) Grade 1 musicianship examinations, and most Level 1 requirements of other examining boards and music teachers' associations. We strongly recommend that teachers consult current syllabi of specific examining boards for their requirements in each grade.

How to Use This Book

Lesson Organization

Each *Sound Advice* lesson contains three parts:

Learning Guide
The Learning Guides explain and illustrate new concepts. When beginning each lesson, you should always study the Learning Guide before completing the Theory Worksheet and the Ear-Training Worksheet.

Theory Worksheet
The Theory Worksheets contain written exercises for both new and review concepts. Your teacher will mark them for you when they are completed.

Ear-Training Worksheet
The Ear-Training Worksheets involve singing melodies and rhythms, identifying intervals, performing melody playbacks/singbacks and rhythm clapbacks/singbacks, and completing dictation activities. Detailed instructions are provided below. You can check your answers to these assignments yourself, using the Ear-Training Answer Key at the back of the book.

Completing the Ear-Training Worksheets

You will need to go online to access the audio tracks for *Sound Advice* Level 1 to complete the Ear-Training Worksheets. In this book, the track numbers for each exercise are identified by an icon in the margin. The instructions for each exercise will be read aloud on the recording for the first three lessons only. Beginning with Lesson 4, you must read the instructions for each question yourself. Take time to read the instructions *before* you listen to the recorded examples.

For sight-singing and rhythmic-reading questions, you should pause the recording and perform each example by yourself first, tapping a steady quarter-note beat with your finger while you sing. To check your accuracy, sing the example a second time while listening to the recording and following along in the answer key.

Sight-singing melodies and rhythms will be played once on the recording. All the other ear-training examples will be played twice, but you may replay them as many times as necessary. On the Ear-Training Worksheets, you will be asked to record the number of times you listened. Your eventual goal is to complete each question after hearing the recorded example just twice.

When you finish an activity, turn immediately to the Ear-Training Answer Key to mark your work. *Do not erase your mistakes and replace them with the correct answers.* Instead, write in the correct answers *above* the errors. If you correct your work this way, you and your teacher will be able to look back at your progress over several lessons and identify areas that need extra practice.

Important: If you make a mistake on an ear-training question, always go back and listen to the recorded example again to make sure you understand the correct answer.

How to Use This Book

Charts and Games

The Charts and Games begin on p. 113. The charts include Note-Value Comparison, Drawing Symbols, Rhythm Jumble, and Song Clue. These charts provide reinforcement for both writing and ear-training activities. Instructions on how to use each chart appear at the top of the chart.

The Games include Rhythm Jumble Reading, Rhythm Jumble Solitaire, Rhythm Jumble Composer and Mad Music. The games provide an opportunity for students to improve their facility in a fun setting.

Suggestions for Daily Ear-Training Practice

Daily practice in ear training is essential for developing total musicianship. Even if you complete your ear-training assignment immediately after your lesson, you should still do a few minutes of ear-training practice every day until your next lesson. If for some reason you finish *Sound Advice* Level 1 but have to wait before you start Level 2, you should continue to practice ear training every day.

Here are some suggestions:

Sing Intervals

One easy way to learn intervals is to relate them to the notes of the major scale. For example, to learn the perfect 5th, sing up the first five notes of a major scale, stop on the fifth note, then sing the first note again. Sing those two notes back and forth to memorize the sound of that interval.

Song clues can be helpful for identifying and singing intervals. On p. 117, there is a chart showing the ascending intervals with several song clue examples. There is also space for you to add your own song clues. If you sing or hum the song clues, you will quickly memorize the sound of the intervals.

To practice singing intervals when the first note is played for you, follow these steps:

1) Play the first note of the interval on your instrument.
2) Hear the second note in your head. (Use a song clue or relate the notes to the major scale.)
3) Sing the second note out loud.
4) Play the second note on your instrument to see if you sang the right pitch.

The process is "play, hear, sing, play."

Sing Rhythms

One of the best ways to practice rhythm is to use the music you are currently playing or singing. Choose a passage to work on, tap the beat (eventually you will *feel* the beat in your body), and play or sing the rhythms. Be sure to feel the regular accent of the time signature. Remember, the goal is to recognize the symbols on the page as familiar patterns of sounds—not to count them out. Regular practice in this manner will greatly improve your sight reading.

You can also use the Rhythm Jumble Chart on p. 115 to practice singing rhythms every day.

How to Use This Book

Play by Ear

Try to play familiar melodies on your instrument without reading from the music. To figure out which note of the scale a melody starts on, sing the tune and hold the *last* note, which may well be the first note of the scale (do). Now compare that last note to the first note of the melody. Are the pitches the same or different? How far apart are they? HINT: Many familiar melodies begin on the fifth scale degree (sol), for example, *Happy Birthday*, *Silent Night*, *Here Comes the Bride*, *Oh Christmas Tree*, and *Amazing Grace*.

Familiar Tune Dictation

Try writing down a familiar melody. To figure out the meter, sing the tune while you tap the beat and listen for the regular accents. To figure out which notes of the scale the melody begins and ends on, use the procedure described under Play by Ear. If you can sing the tune using pitch syllables, you should be able to write it starting on any note you choose. Compare your written version with the printed music, if you have a copy.

Extra Sight Singing

You can use the Ear-Training Answer Key for extra practice in singing melodies and rhythms. When you sight sing these "answers," follow the same procedure you use when reading melodies and rhythms in the ear-training assignments.

Lesson 1

Learning Guide

I am your professor. I will be your guide throughout this book. Be sure to follow my advice when I offer you a suggestion!

Beat and Tempo

If you take your pulse or sit quietly and feel your heartbeat, you will notice that it has a **steady beat**. Each beat of your pulse can represent one beat of sound. In music, "pulse" means the same thing as "beat." To be a good musician, you must be able to maintain a steady beat.

Your heartbeats might be fast if you have been running, or slow if you have been sleeping. In music, we use the word **tempo** to describe how fast or slow the beats are moving.

Notes

The symbols used to represent music on paper are called **notes**. Most notes are made up of a notehead and a stem. Some stems have flags.

Noteheads

Noteheads with stems

Stems with flags

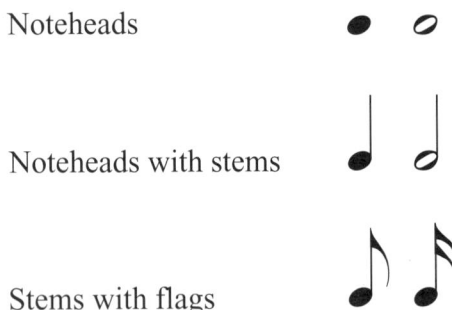

10   Lesson 1 Learning Guide   Sound Advice Level 1

Learning Guide — Lesson 1

Duration: Quarter Notes and Half Notes

When we talk about the length of a note we are talking about its **duration**. Some notes are long, other notes are short. You can tell how long to hold a note by the way it looks.

The Quarter Note

The notes below are called **quarter notes**. Each quarter note represents *one* beat of sound. Tap a steady beat with your finger while you sing these quarter notes:

Sing: ta   ta   ta   ta
Tap: ✗   ✗   ✗   ✗

The Half Note

The notes below are called **half notes**. Each half note represents *two* beats of sound. Tap a steady beat while you sing these half notes:

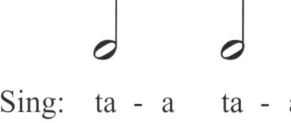

Sing: ta - a   ta - a
Tap: ✗   ✗   ✗   ✗

Rhythm Jumble

Now you have learned two kinds of notes: quarter notes and half notes. Turn to the Rhythm Jumble Chart on p. 115 and circle these two note values.

Each time you learn a new rhythmic unit, you can circle it on this chart. In your daily practice, sing all the circled units several times while you tap a steady beat.

LESSON 1

Theory Worksheet

1 Trace the quarter note below, then draw five of your own. Tap a steady beat and sing this quarter-note pattern several times.

 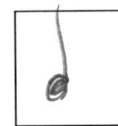   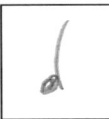 

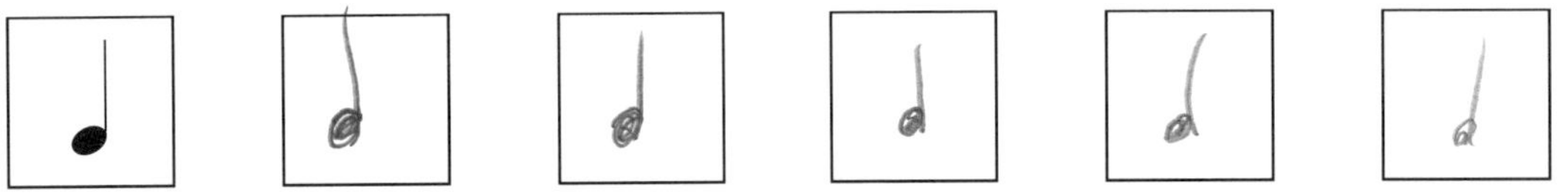

2 Trace the half note below, then draw five of your own. Tap a steady beat and sing this half-note pattern several times. Make sure the sound of each half note lasts for two beats.

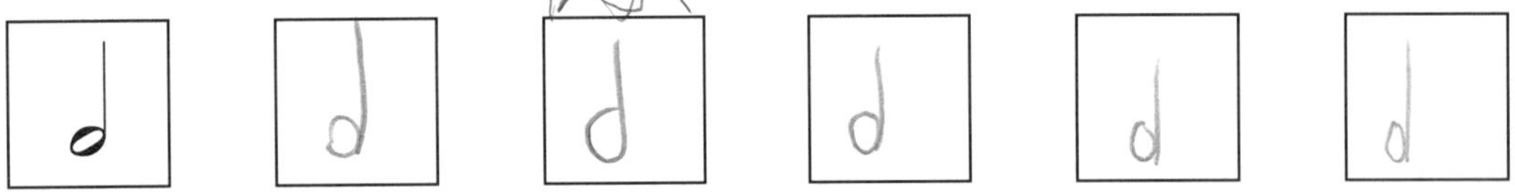

3 Use quarter and half notes to write your own rhythmic pattern. Tap a steady beat and sing your pattern several times.

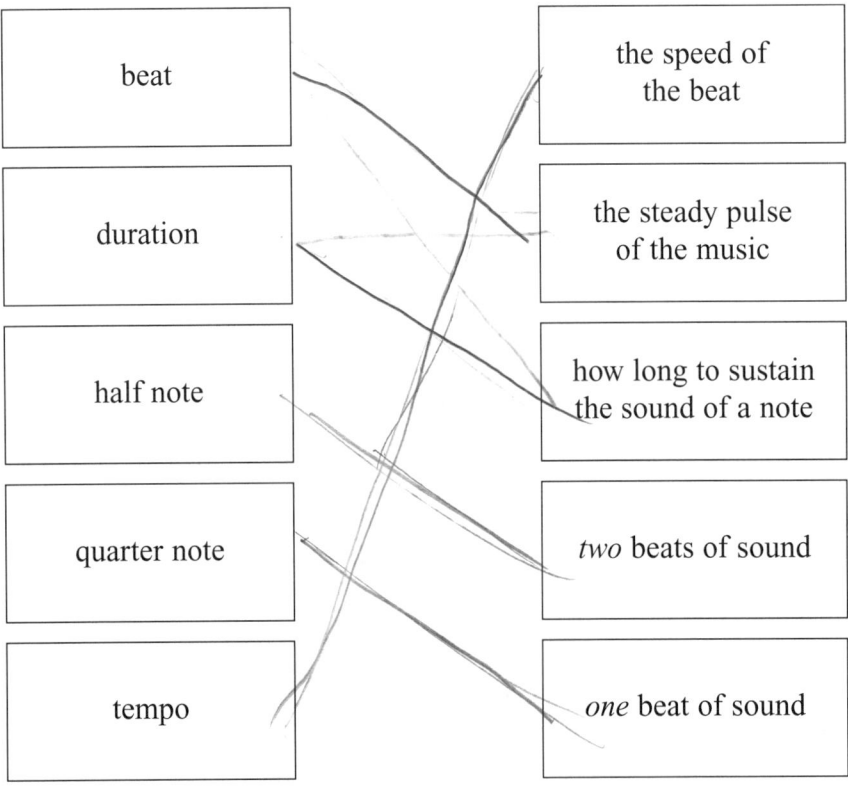

4 Draw a line from each word on the left to its definition on the right.

beat	the speed of the beat
duration	the steady pulse of the music
half note	how long to sustain the sound of a note
quarter note	*two* beats of sound
tempo	*one* beat of sound

LESSON 1

Ear-Training Worksheet

Before completing the ear-training assignments, turn to p. 7 and read the instructions.

Track 1

1 **Tempo Identification:** Tap a steady beat while you listen to each example. Identify the tempo of each example as slow, medium, or fast.

a) ☒ slow   b) ☐ slow   c) ☐ slow
   ☐ medium   ☐ medium   ☒ medium
   ☐ fast   ☒ fast   ☐ fast

Track 2

2 **Rhythmic Reading:**
a) Pause the recording. Sing the following rhythmic pattern while you tap a steady quarter-note beat.
b) Turn to the answer key and sing along with the recording.

Track 3

3 **Rhythmic Reading:**
a) Pause the recording. Sing the following rhythmic pattern while you tap a steady quarter-note beat.
b) Turn to the answer key and sing along with the recording.

Track 4

4 **Rhythmic Identification:** Identify the correct notation for the rhythmic pattern you hear. The pattern will be played twice.

☐    ☒

Track 5

5 **Rhythmic Dictation:** Listen to the following rhythmic pattern, then add the correct noteheads to the stems below. The pattern will be played twice.

Always tap the beat while you listen!

ex. 4 + 5 not on theory lab computers. (am)

Sound Advice Level 1   Lesson 1 Ear-Training Worksheet   13

Learning Guide

Pitch

We use the word **pitch** to describe how high or low a note sounds. On a keyboard, the pitch of the notes gets higher as you move to the right, and lower as you move to the left.

Lower-pitched notes ☜   ☞ Higher-pitched notes

Staff

Notes are written on a **staff**. A staff has *five* lines and *four* spaces.

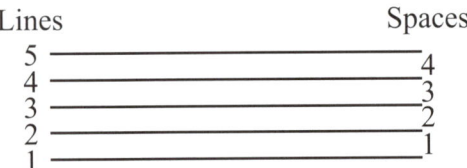

Line Notes

The notes below are called **line notes**. The staff lines run through the middle of the noteheads:

Reading from left to right, the pitch of these notes goes up and then down.

higher pitch

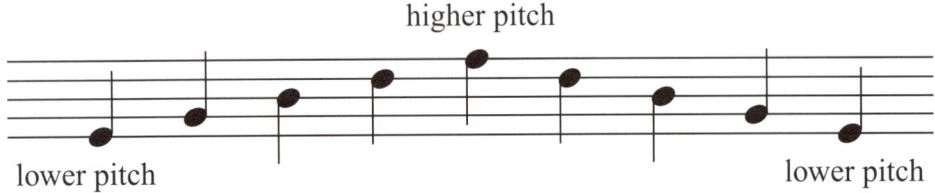

lower pitch   lower pitch

Learning Guide

LESSON 2

Space Notes

The notes below are called **space notes.** The noteheads sit in the spaces between the lines:

Stem Direction

All notes look like either p's or d's, as in the words **pay day**.

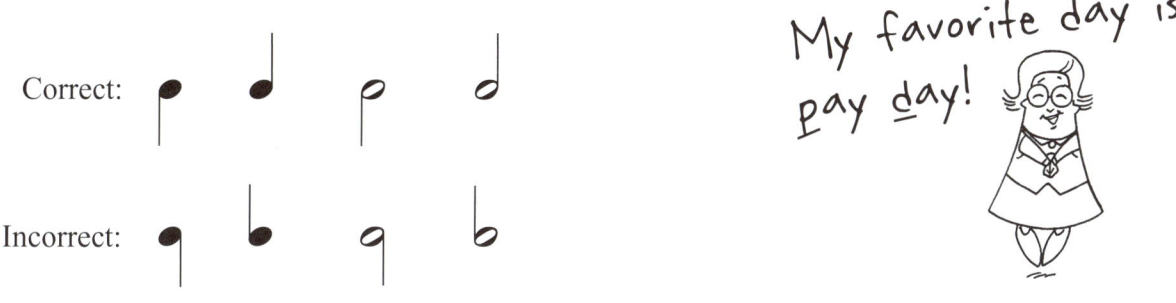

When a note is written below the middle line, the stem goes up. When a note is written above the middle line, the stem goes down.

When a note is written on the middle line, the stem can go either up or down.

We will learn more about stem direction in Lesson 8.

Sound Advice Level 1   Lesson 2 Learning Guide   15

LESSON 2 Theory Worksheet

1 Circle the notes that have stems going in the wrong direction.

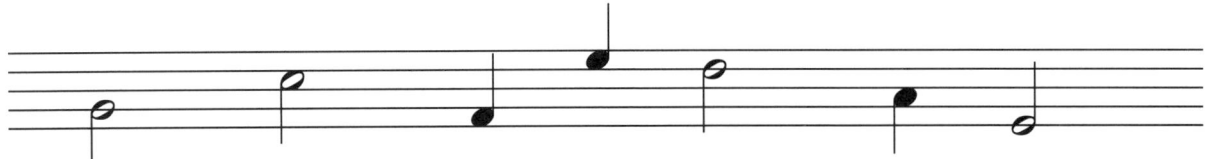

2 Add stems to these noteheads to create quarter notes and half notes. Think of **pay** **d**ay.

3 Using quarter notes, draw five different space notes anywhere on the staff below. Circle the note that has the highest pitch. Make sure the stems go in the correct direction.

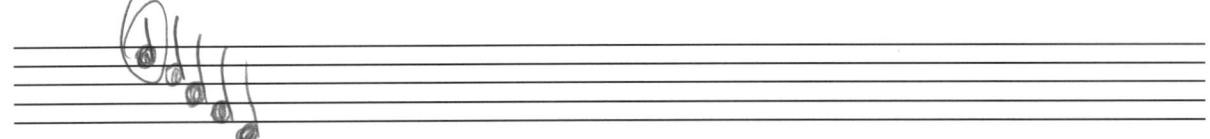

4 Using half notes, draw five different line notes anywhere on the staff below. Circle the note that has the lowest pitch. Make sure the stems go in the correct direction.

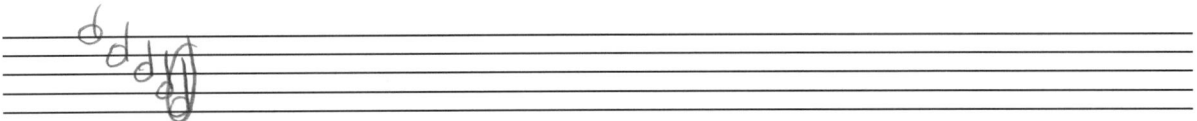

5 Use quarter notes and half notes to write your own rhythmic pattern below. Use at least eight notes. Tap a steady beat and sing your pattern several times.

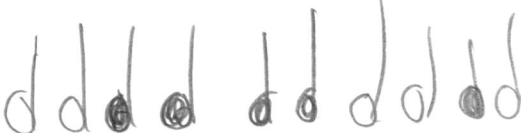

LESSON 2
Ear-Training Worksheet

1. Pitch Direction: You will hear a pair of notes. Identify the pitch of the *second* note as higher than, lower than, or the same as the pitch of the first note. Each example will be played twice.

a) ■ higher
☐ lower
☐ same

b) ☐ higher
☐ lower
■ same

2. Pitch Direction: You will hear a pattern of three notes. Identify whether the notes go up, go down, or repeat. The pattern will be played twice.

a) ■ up
☐ down
☐ repeat

b) ☐ up
☐ down
■ repeat

c) ☐ up
■ down
☐ repeat

3. Rhythmic Reading:
a) Pause the recording. Sing the following rhythmic pattern while you tap a steady quarter-note beat.
b) Turn to the answer key and sing along with the recording.

4. Rhythmic Reading:
a) Pause the recording. Sing the following rhythmic pattern while you tap a steady quarter-note beat.
b) Turn to the answer key and sing along with the recording.

5. Rhythmic Dictation: Listen to the following rhythmic pattern. Then add the correct noteheads to the stems below. The pattern will be played twice.

Always tap the beat while you listen!

Sound Advice Level 1   Lesson 2 Ear-Training Worksheet   17

Learning Guide

Rhythmic Dictation

In music, writing down—or notating—what you hear is called **dictation**. This is a useful skill for any musician. The first type of dictation you will learn is rhythmic dictation. When you do rhythmic dictation, you only write the rhythm, even if the example you hear is a melody.

When you do rhythmic dictation, there are three steps to follow. We'll use this rhythmic pattern as an example:

1 Write a stem for each sound you hear. Start from the top and draw down, like this: ↓
Write the stems close together when you hear short notes. Write the stems farther apart when you hear longer notes, like this:

2 Sing the pattern back to yourself from memory and follow the stems you have written. Try to remember which notes were longer. In this example, the longer note lasted for two beats. Add the notehead for a half note where you heard the long note, like this:

3 Add noteheads to the quarter notes to finish your dictation.

Theory Worksheet — Lesson 3

1 Using half notes, draw five different space notes that get lower in pitch.

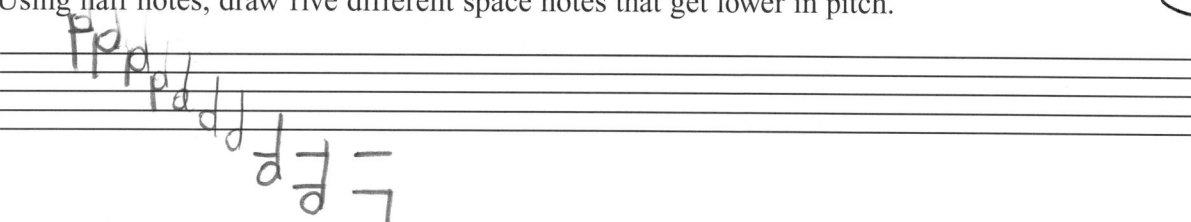

2 Using quarter notes, draw five different line notes that get higher in pitch.

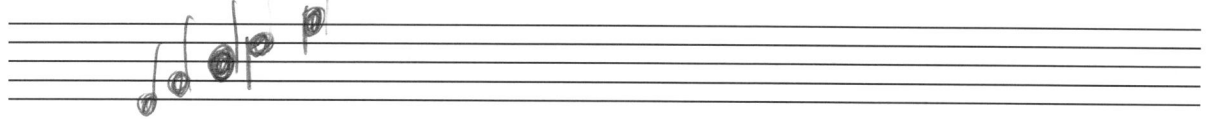

3 Circle the notes that have stems going in the wrong direction.

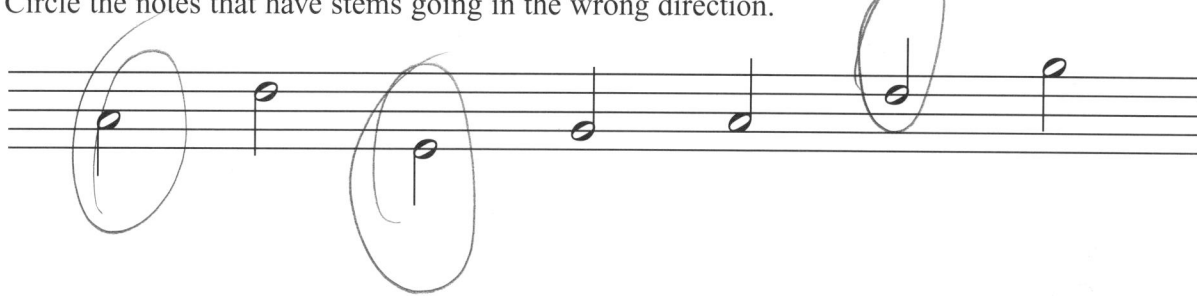

4 Add stems to the following noteheads to create half notes. Think of **p**ay **d**ay.

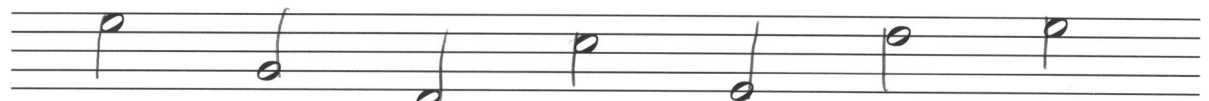

5 Use a combination of quarter notes and half notes to write your own rhythmic pattern below. Use at least eight notes. Tap a steady beat and sing your pattern several times.

Sound Advice Level 1 — Lesson 3 Theory Worksheet

LESSON 3 — Ear-Training Worksheet

 1 **Rhythmic Reading:**

a) Pause the recording. Sing the following rhythmic pattern while you tap a steady quarter-note beat.

b) Turn to the answer key and sing along with the recording.

 2 **Rhythm Singback/Clapback:** Sing, tap, or clap the rhythmic pattern you hear from memory. The pattern will be played twice, but you may listen as many times as you need. Record the number of times you listened.

 Your goal is to memorize the pattern after it is played twice.

 3 **Rhythmic Dictation:** Write the rhythmic pattern you hear in the space below. Listen to the example as many times as you need. The pattern will be played twice.

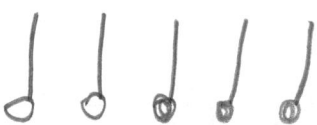

Write it down as you hear it!

 4 **Pitch Direction:** You will hear a pattern of four notes. Identify whether the notes go up, go down, or repeat. The pattern will be played twice.

a) ☐ up
☒ down
☐ repeat

b) ☒ up
☐ down
☐ repeat

c) ☐ up
☐ down
☒ repeat

5 **Pitch Identification:** Identify the correct notation for the pitch pattern you hear.

a) ☐    ☒    ☐

b) ☒    ☐   ☐

20 — Lesson 3 Ear-Training Worksheet — Sound Advice Level 1

Learning Guide

The Music Alphabet

The music alphabet has seven letters: **A B C D E F G**. These seven letters repeat over and over again. The letter after **G** is **A,** not **H**.

To read music easily, you must be able to go up and down the alphabet starting on any letter.

The Keyboard

On a full-sized piano keyboard, the white keys are named from left to right, starting with A. There are only seven *different* white keys on the keyboard. Like the letters of the music alphabet, these seven key names are repeated over and over again.

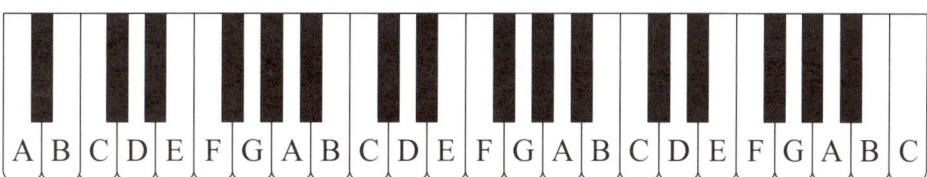

The Treble Clef and Treble Staff

This symbol is called a **treble clef**:

The treble clef is used for **higher-pitched notes**, such as those played by the right hand on the piano, or by higher instruments like the violin and the flute.

The treble clef is sometimes called the **G clef** because it marks the note G on the staff. When a staff has a treble clef, the staff is called a **treble staff**.

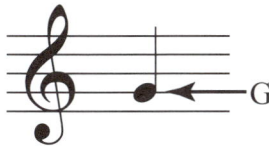

Sound Advice Level 1 — Lesson 4 Learning Guide — 21

LESSON 4 Learning Guide

Notes that move from *line to space*, or *space to line*, are named in music-alphabet order. When the notes go up in pitch, you spell forward (A–B–C–D–E). When the notes go down in pitch, you spell backwards (E–D–C–B–A).

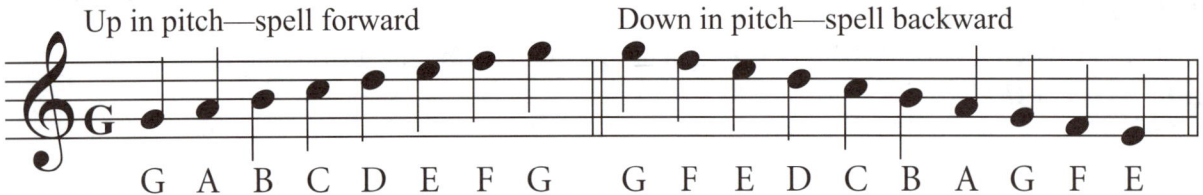

How to Draw a Treble Clef

1 Draw a line down with a curve at the bottom.

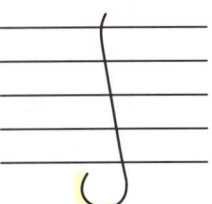

2 Count up four lines and make a dot.

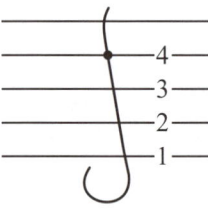

3 Make your first loop.

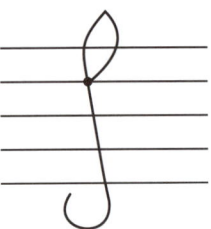

4 Make your second loop.

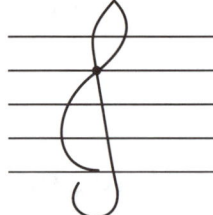

5 Make your third loop and stop just below the second line.

Learning Guide

LESSON 4

Ledger Lines

If you run out of regular staff lines, you can add another short line of your own. These extra lines are called **ledger lines**.

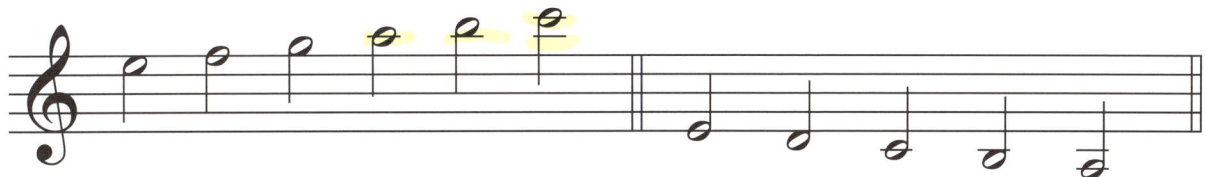

This note is **Middle C**. It is written on a ledger line below the treble staff. On a piano keyboard, Middle C is in the center.

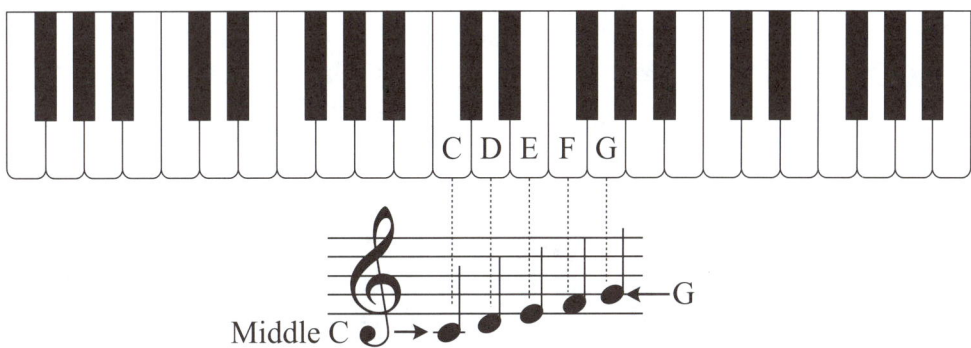

Treble-Staff Landmarks

Landmarks are notes that are easily recognized and memorized. There are two treble-staff landmarks: **Middle C** and **Treble G**. To name notes in the treble staff, you can:

Spell up or down the music alphabet from Middle C.

Spell up or down the music alphabet from Treble G.

Sound Advice Level 1   Lesson 4 Learning Guide   23

LESSON 4 — Theory Worksheet

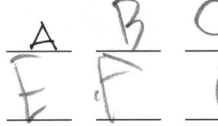

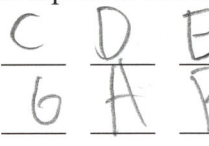

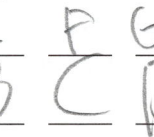

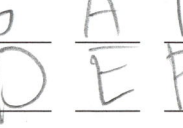

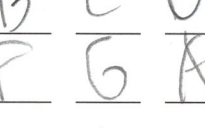

1 Write the music alphabet starting on A. You will need to repeat it several times.

A B C D E F G A B C D (continue on next line)
E F G A B C D E F G A

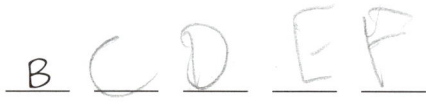

2 Write the missing letters in the blanks below, going *up* the music alphabet.

A B C D E   B C D E F
C D E F G   F G A B C

3 Write the missing letters in the blanks below, going *down* the music alphabet. (HINT: Spell backwards!)

G F E D C B A G

4 Name all the white keys on this keyboard.

F G A B C D E F G A B C D E F G A B C D E F G A B

5 Trace the treble clef below, then draw five of your own. For extra practice, turn to the Drawing Symbols Chart on p. 114 and draw some more.

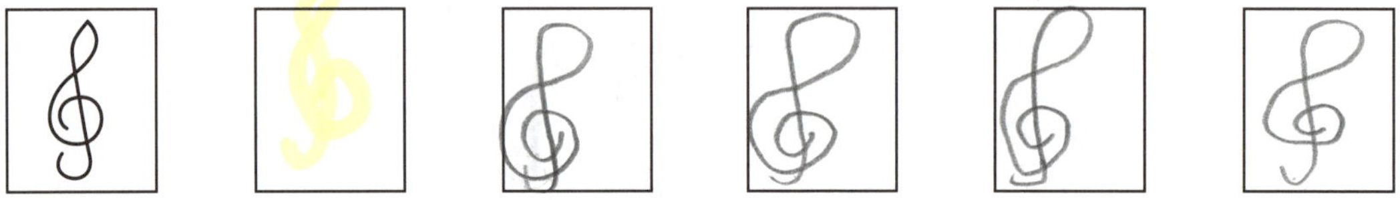

6 Draw five treble clefs on the staff below. The first one is done for you to trace.

Theory Worksheet — Lesson 4

7 Draw and name seven half notes moving up on the staff. The first notehead has been provided.

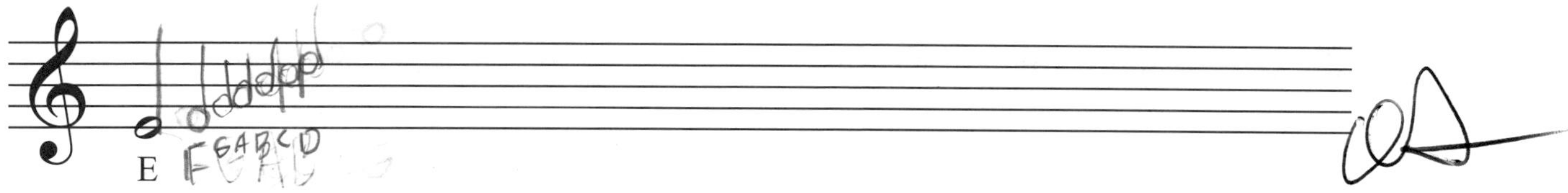

E F G A B C D

8 Name the following treble-staff notes. Draw a line from each note to its corresponding white key on the keyboard.

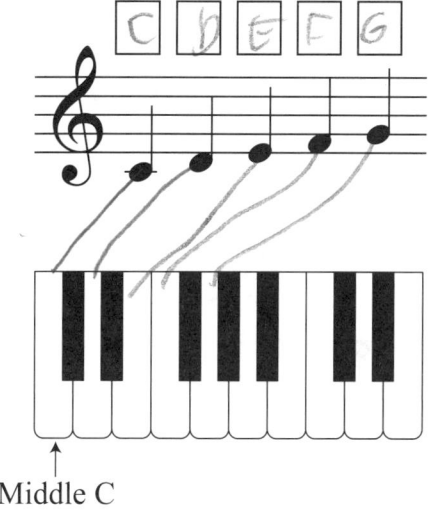

C D E F G

Middle C

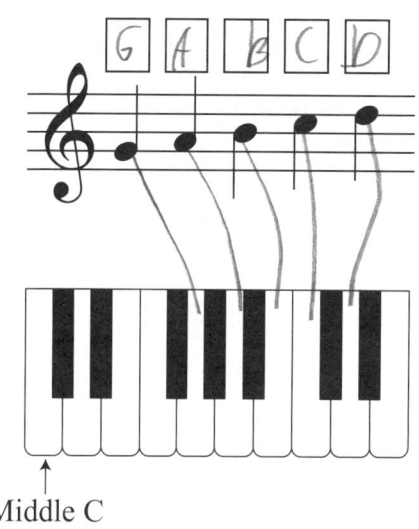

G A B C D

Middle C

G F E D C

Middle C

G A B A G

Middle C

EGBDF FACE ACEG GBDFA

LESSON 4: Ear-Training Worksheet

Beginning with this lesson, the instructions will no longer be read aloud on the recording. Read each question carefully before you listen.

 1 **Pitch Identification:** Identify the correct notation for the pitch pattern you hear.

a)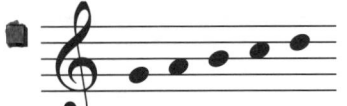

b)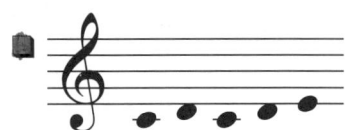

 2 **Rhythmic Identification:** Identify the correct notation for the rhythmic pattern you hear.

a) ☐ 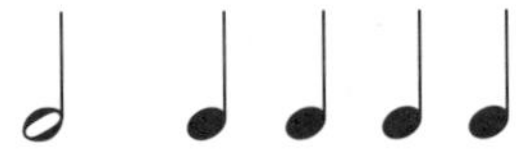    ■

b) ■    ☐

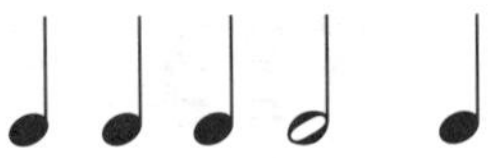

 3 **Rhythmic Reading:**

a) Pause the recording. Sing the following rhythmic pattern while you tap a steady quarter-note beat.

b) Turn to the answer key and sing along with the recording.

 4 **Rhythm Singback/Clapback:** Sing, tap, or clap the rhythmic pattern you hear from memory. Listen to the example as many times as you need.

 5 **Rhythmic Dictation:** Write the rhythmic pattern you hear in the space below. Listen to the example as many times as you need.

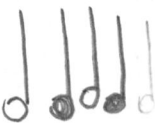

Write it down as you hear it!

Learning Guide

The Bass Clef and Bass Staff

This symbol is called a **bass clef**. 𝄢

The bass clef is used for the **lower-pitched notes** such as those played by the left hand on the piano, or by lower-pitched instruments like the cello and the tuba.

The bass clef is sometimes called the **F clef** because it marks the note F on the staff. When a staff has a bass clef, the staff is called a **bass staff**.

F

How to Draw a Bass Clef

1 Draw a dot on line 4.

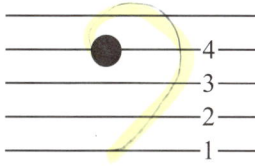

2 Make a curve, stopping just below line 2.

3 Write dots in spaces 3 and 4.

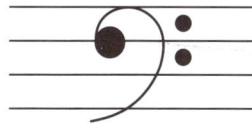

LESSON 5 Learning Guide

Bass-Staff Landmarks

There are two bass-staff landmarks: **Middle C** and **Bass F.** To name notes in the bass staff, you can:

Spell up or down the music alphabet from Middle C.

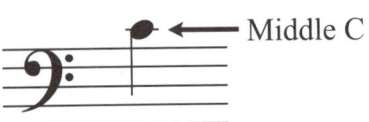 ← Middle C

In the bass staff, Middle C is written on a ledger line above the staff.

Spell up or down the music alphabet from Bass F.

A Closer Look at Middle C

Compare these two Middle C's. They are written in different clefs, but they represent the same pitch and the same key on a piano keyboard.

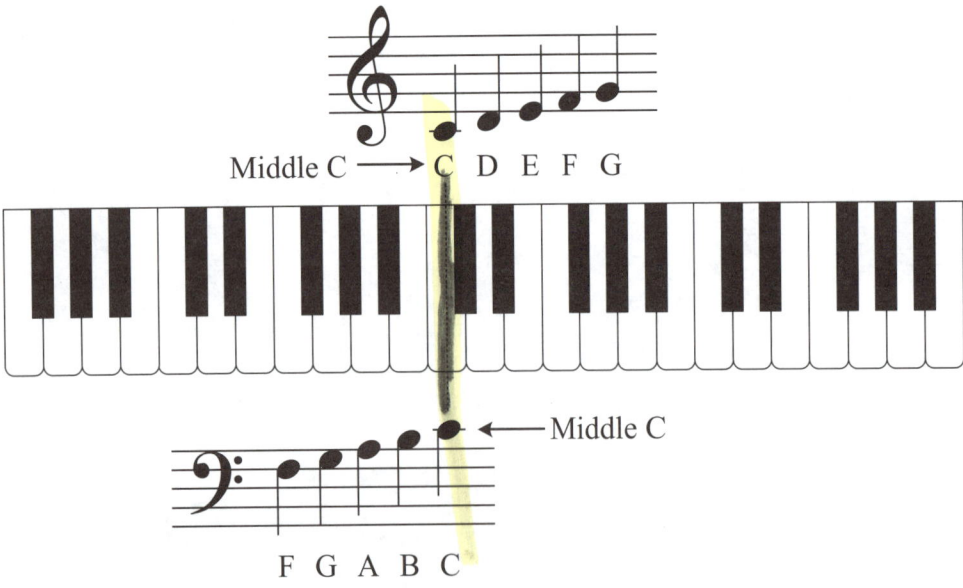

28   Lesson 5 Learning Guide   Sound Advice Level 1

Theory Worksheet — Lesson 5

1 Trace the bass clef below, then draw five of your own. For extra practice, turn to the Drawing Symbols Chart on p. 114 and draw some more.

  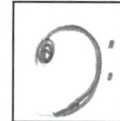 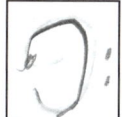  

2 Draw five bass clefs on the staff below. The first one is done for you to trace.

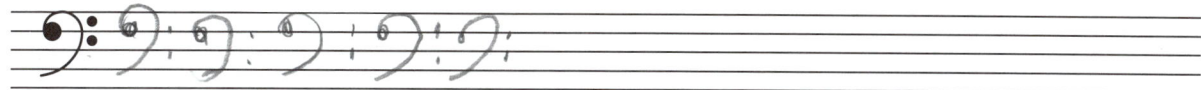

3 Name the following bass-staff notes. Draw a line from each note to its corresponding white key on the keyboard.

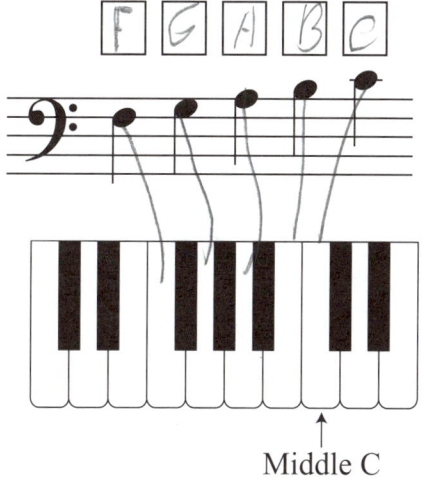
Middle C

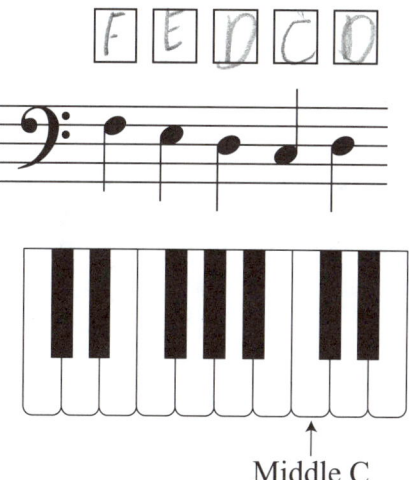
Middle C

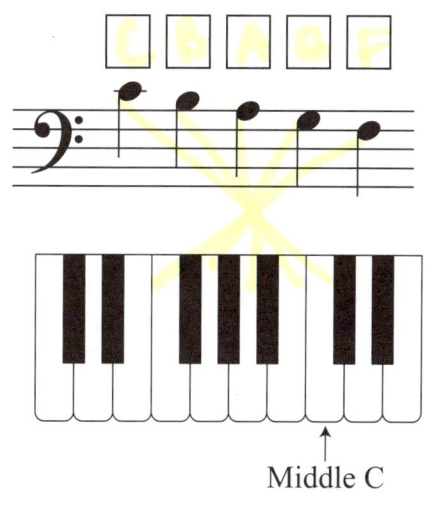
Middle C

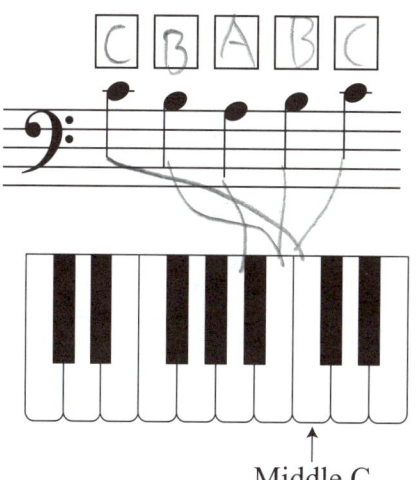
Middle C

Sound Advice Level 1 — Lesson 5 Theory Worksheet

LESSON 5 Theory Worksheet

4 Name the following treble-staff notes. Draw a line from each note to its corresponding white key on the keyboard.

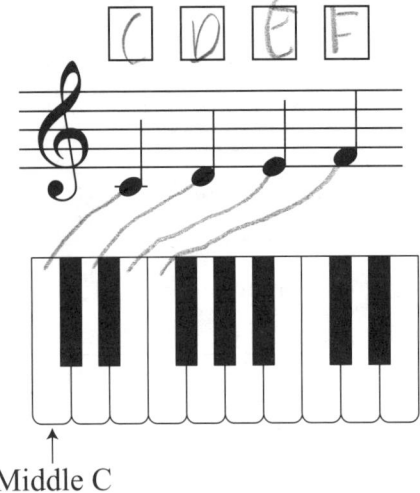
C D E F

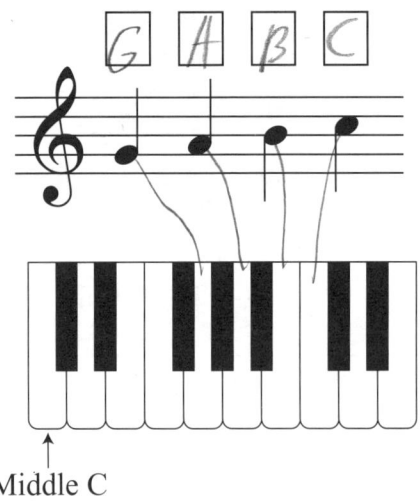
G A B C

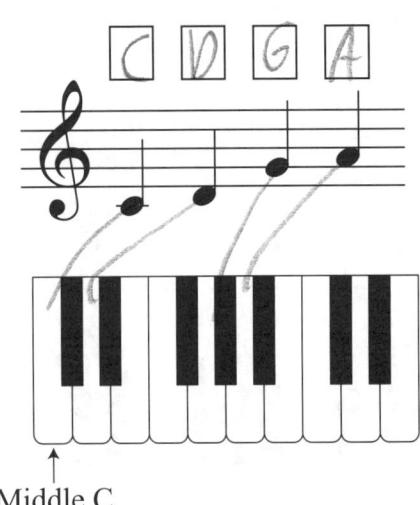
C D G A

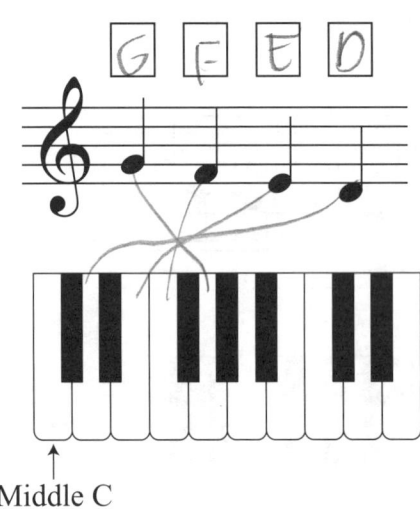
G F E D

5 Write the missing letters in the blanks below, going *up* the music alphabet.

B C D E F G A B

D E F G A B C D

6 Write the missing letters in the blanks below, going *down* the music alphabet.

F E D C B A G F

C B A G F E D C

Ear-Training Worksheet

LESSON 5

 1 **Pitch Identification:** Identify the correct notation for the pitch pattern you hear.

a) ☐    ☐    ■

b) ■    ☐    ☐

 2 **Rhythmic Identification:** Identify the correct notation for the rhythmic pattern you hear.

a) ■    ☐

b) ☐    ■

 3 **Rhythmic Reading:**
a) Pause the recording. Sing the following rhythmic pattern while you tap a steady quarter-note beat.
b) Turn to the answer key and sing along with the recording.

 4 **Rhythm Singback/Clapback:** Sing, tap, or clap the rhythmic pattern you hear from memory. Listen to the example as many times as you need.

 5 **Rhythmic Dictation:** Write the rhythmic pattern you hear in the space below. Listen to the example as many times as you need.

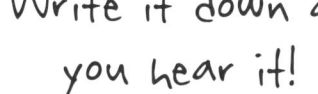

Sound Advice Level 1 — Lesson 5 Ear-Training Worksheet — 31

Learning Guide

The Grand Staff

Keyboard players have to read two clefs at the same time. The staff below has eleven lines. The middle line is Middle C. It would be hard to read music written on a big staff like this.

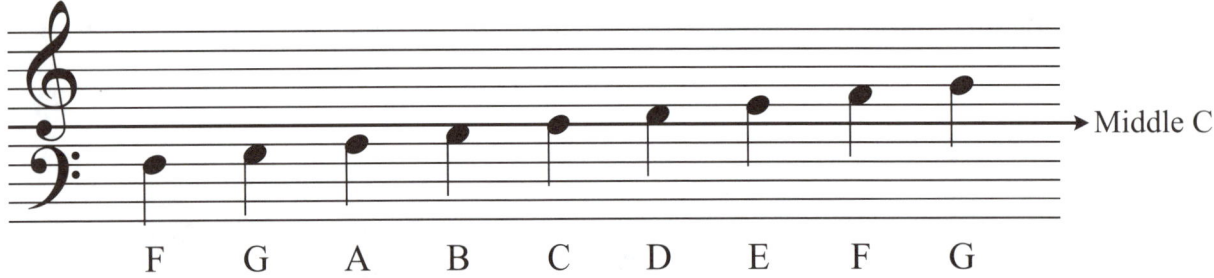

If we divide the eleven lines into two groups of five lines, the music is easier to read. We use a ledger line when we need to write Middle C.

This divided staff is called a **grand staff**. A grand staff consists of a treble staff and a bass staff. A bracket on the left joins the two staffs.

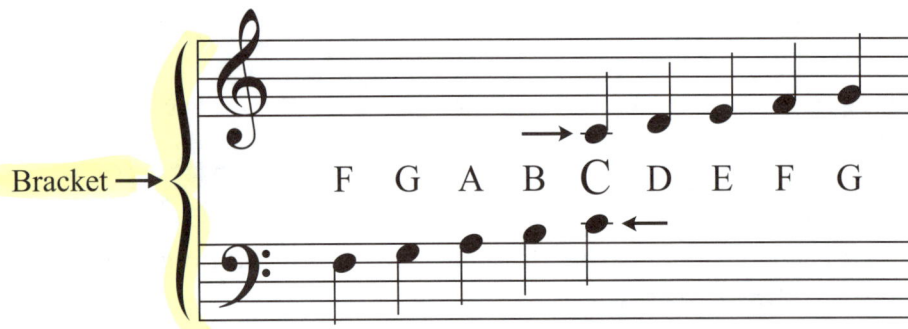

Middle C on the Grand Staff

Middle C can be written on either the bass staff or the treble staff. To make sure you understand this, play the following notes on a keyboard.

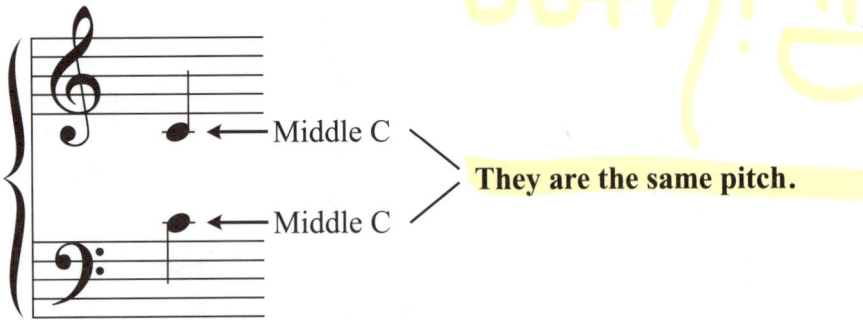

They are the same pitch.

32   Lesson 6 Learning Guide   Sound Advice Level 1

Theory Worksheet — Lesson 6

1 Name the following treble staff notes. Draw a line from each note to its corresponding white key on the keyboard below.

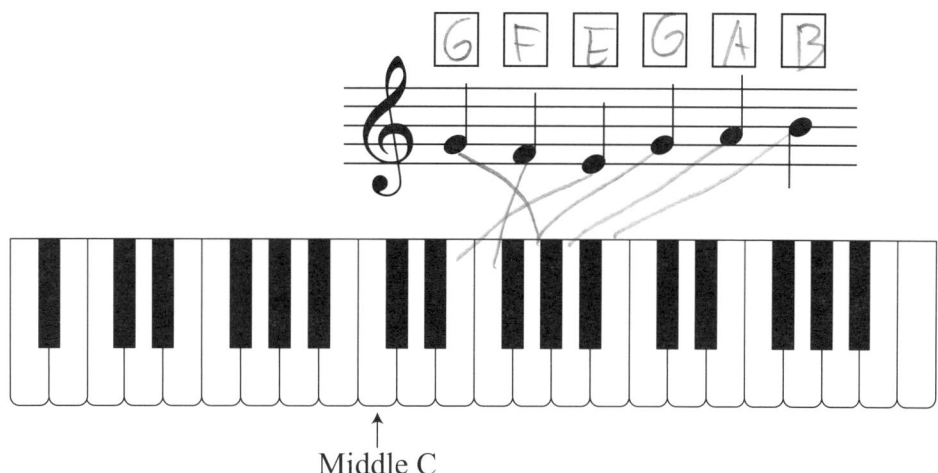

G F E G A B

2 Name the following bass staff notes. Draw a line from each note to its corresponding white key on the keyboard below.

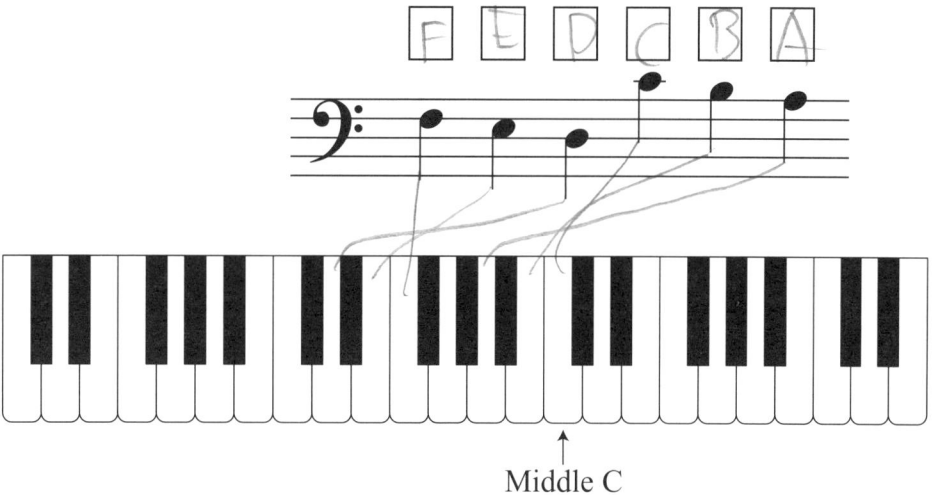

F E D C B A

3 Name the following notes.

C D E   G F E

F G A   C B A

Sound Advice Level 1 — Lesson 6 Theory Worksheet — 33

LESSON 6 Ear-Training Worksheet

 1 **Pitch Identification:** Identify the correct notation for the pitch pattern you hear.

a)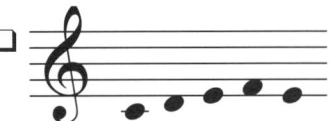

b)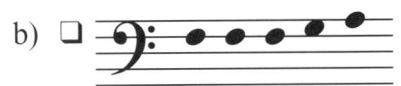

 2 **Rhythmic Reading:**
a) Pause the recording. Sing the following rhythmic pattern while you tap a steady quarter-note beat.

b) Turn to the answer key and sing along with the recording.

 3 **Rhythm Clapback:** Clap the *rhythm* of the melody you hear from memory. Record the number of times you listened. Your goal is to memorize the *rhythm* after the melody is played twice.

 4 **Rhythm Clapback:** Clap the *rhythm* of the melody you hear from memory. Record the number of times you listened. Your goal is to memorize the *rhythm* after the melody is played twice.

 5 **Rhythmic Dictation:** Write the rhythmic pattern you hear in the space below. Listen to the example as many times as you need.

34   Lesson 6 Ear-Training Worksheet   Sound Advice Level 1

Learning Guide

Naming Notes on the Grand Staff

To name notes on the grand staff quickly, you can use any of the landmarks you learned in Lessons 4 and 5. You can also spell up from **A**—the lowest space in the bass staff.

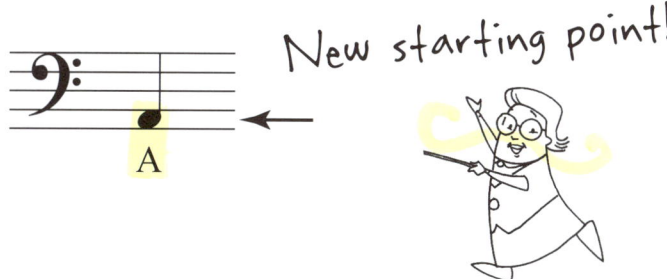

This new starting point is helpful for naming low notes on the bass staff.

On the grand staff, you can step up from the lowest space in the bass staff (A)—one note at a time (space, line, space, line, etc.)—spelling the music alphabet right through both clefs.

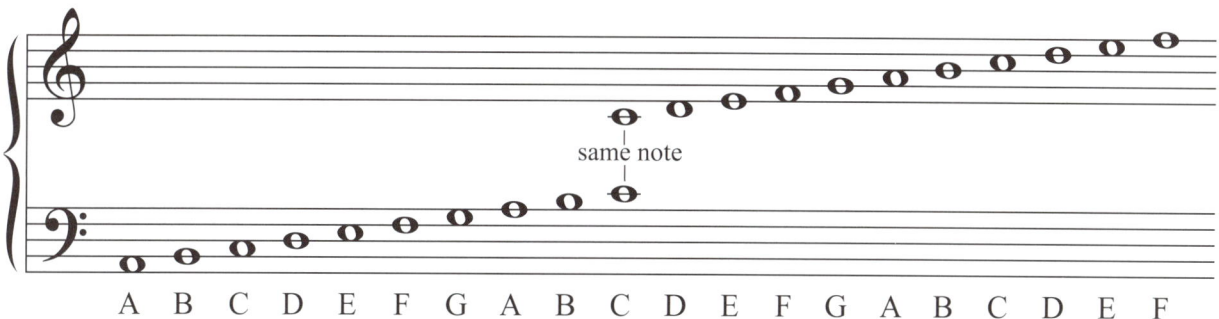

Mad Music

Mad Music is a note-naming game with three levels of difficulty. From now on, many of your theory worksheets will include space for you to record three Mad Music scores. This means that part of your homework for that lesson is to play Mad Music at least three times. When you have mastered the third level of Mad Music, you do not have to record any more scores.

Beginning with Mad Music Level A on p. 119, try to name as many notes on the sheet as you can within two minutes. Full instructions on how to play Mad Music are on p. 118.

Sound Advice Level 1   Lesson 7 Learning Guide   35

LESSON 7 Theory Worksheet

1 Name the following notes.

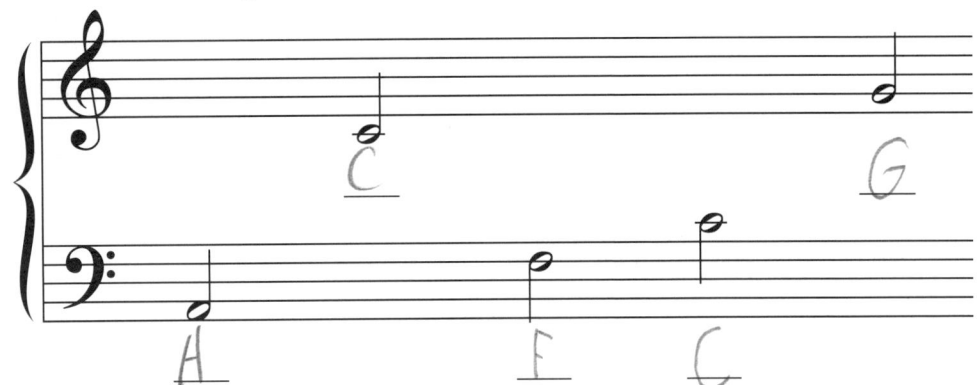

2 Name the following notes.

3 Add the missing treble clef or bass clef to each example below.

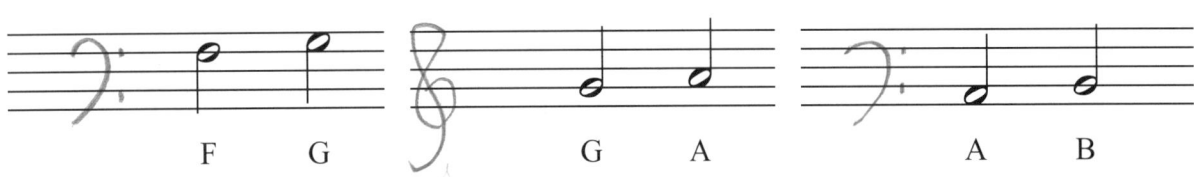

4 Mad Music Scores

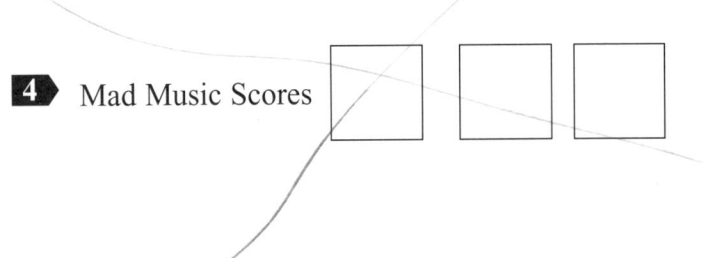

Ear-Training Worksheet

LESSON 7

Track 31

1) Melodic Identification: Identify the correct notation for the melody you hear.

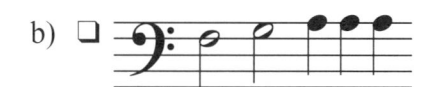

a)

b)

Track 32

2) Rhythmic Reading:
a) Pause the recording. Sing the following rhythmic pattern while you tap a steady quarter-note beat.
b) Turn to the answer key and sing along with the recording.

Track 33

3) Rhythmic Identification: Identify the correct notation for the rhythmic pattern you hear.

a)

b)

Track 34

4) Rhythm Singback/Clapback: Sing, tap, or clap the rhythmic pattern you hear from memory. Listen to the example as many times as you need.

I LISTENED ☐ TIMES

Track 35

5) Rhythmic Dictation: Write the rhythmic pattern you hear in the space below. Listen to the example as many times as you need.

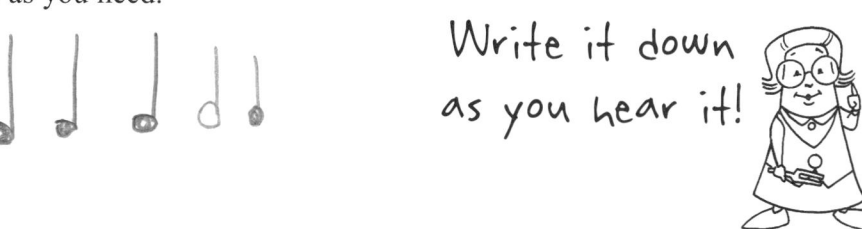

Write it down as you hear it!

Sound Advice Level 1 — Lesson 7 Ear-Training Worksheet

Lesson 8

Learning Guide

The Eighth Note ♪

These two notes are **eighth notes**: ♪♪

They look like quarter notes but they have "flags" on their stems.

Two eighth notes that are joined together look like this: ♫

When two eighth notes are joined as *one* rhythmic unit, we replace the flags with a beam that connects the two stems:

♪ ♪ = ♫

A pair of eighth notes lasts for *one* quarter-note beat: ♫ = 1 beat

A single eighth note lasts for *half* of one quarter-note beat: ♪ = ½ a beat

Tap a steady quarter-note beat while you sing these eighth notes:

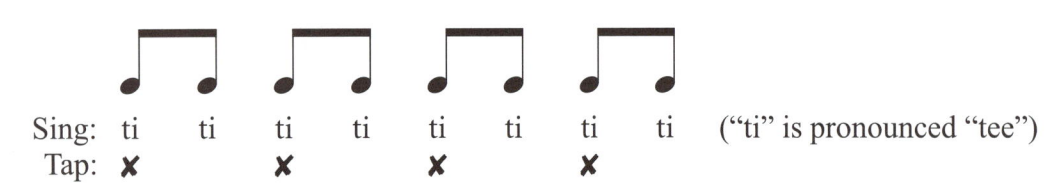

♫ ♫ ♫ ♫

Sing: ti ti   ti ti   ti ti   ti ti   ("ti" is pronounced "tee")
Tap: ✗   ✗   ✗   ✗

Tap the quarter-note beat only!

Turn to the Rhythm Jumble Chart on p. 115 and circle the pair of eighth notes.

Rhythm Jumble

Now that you have learned several different rhythmic units, you are ready to play Rhythm Jumble. For instructions, see the Rhythm Jumble Chart on p. 115.

Learning Guide

LESSON 8

Rhythmic Dictation with Eighth Notes

Now that you have learned about eighth notes, you should listen for them in dictation exercises. Here is an example of a rhythmic pattern that includes eighth notes.

Here are three steps you can follow.

1 Write a stem for each sound you hear. Put the stems close together when you hear eighth notes, and farther apart for longer notes, like this:

2 Sing the rhythmic pattern back to yourself from memory while you follow the stems. Try to remember which notes were longer and which notes were shorter. For this rhythm, add a half-note head for the longer note, and join the two shorter notes with a beam.

3 Add noteheads to the quarter notes and eighth notes to complete your dictation.

Sound Advice Level 1   Lesson 8 Learning Guide   39

LESSON 8 Learning Guide

A Closer Look at Stem Direction

When a note stands alone on the middle line of the staff, the stem can go up or down, but down is always preferred.

note stands alone = stem down

When a middle-line note is beamed to another note, its stem will follow the same direction as the other note.

In a group of beamed notes, all the stems go in the same direction as the note that is the farthest from the middle line.

This F wins!

This C wins!

40   Lesson 8 Learning Guide   Sound Advice Level 1

LESSON 8

Theory Worksheet

1 Name the following notes. Draw a line from each note to its corresponding white key on the keyboard.

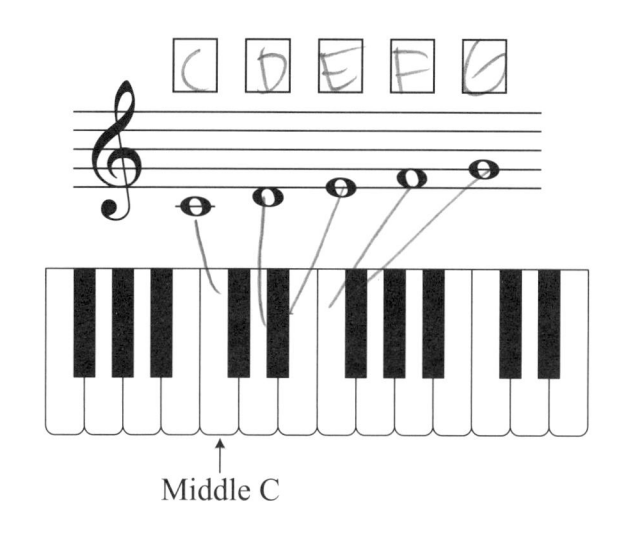

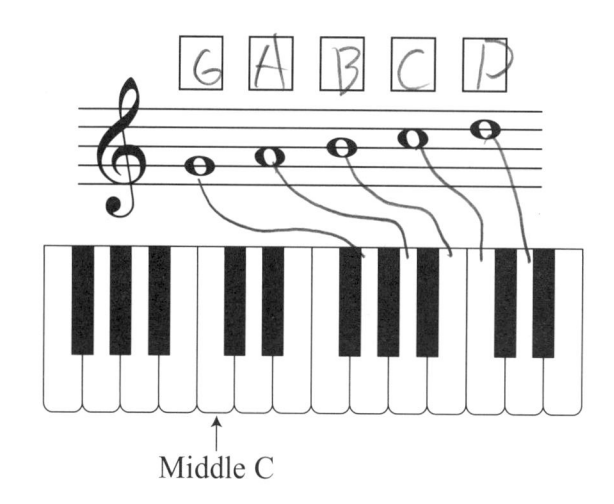

C D E F G

G A B C D

Middle C   Middle C

2 Add stems to the noteheads below.

3 Write the *single* note that equals the duration of the pair of notes below.

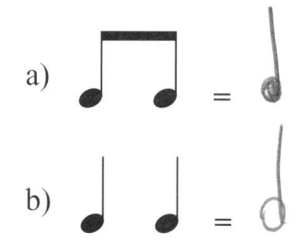

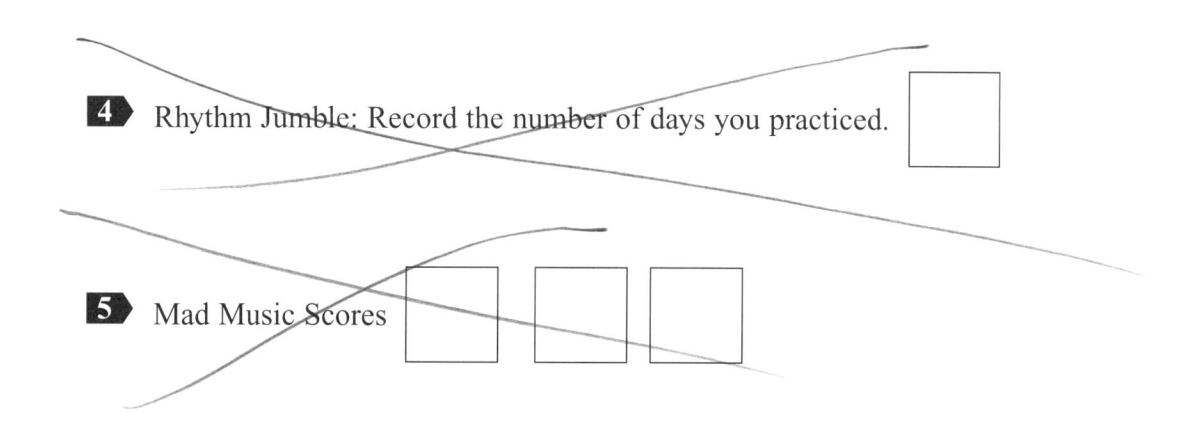

a)
b)

4 Rhythm Jumble: Record the number of days you practiced.

5 Mad Music Scores

Sound Advice Level 1 — Lesson 8 Theory Worksheet

LESSON 8

Ear-Training Worksheet

Track 36

1) Rhythmic Reading:

a) Pause the recording. Sing the following rhythmic pattern while you tap a steady quarter-note beat.

b) Turn to the answer key and sing along with the recording.

Track 37

2) Rhythmic Reading:

a) Pause the recording. Sing the following rhythmic pattern while you tap a steady quarter-note beat.

b) Turn to the answer key and sing along with the recording.

Track 38

3) Rhythmic Identification: Identify the correct notation for the rhythmic pattern you hear.

a)

b)

Track 39

4) Rhythmic Dictation: Add the missing notes under the brackets. Each pattern will be played twice.

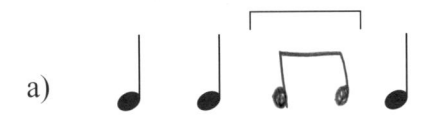

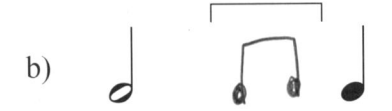

a)

b)

c)

Write it down as you hear it!

Track 40

5) Rhythmic Dictation: Write the rhythmic pattern you hear in the space below. Listen to the example as many times as you need.

42   Lesson 8 Ear-Training Worksheet   Sound Advice Level 1

Learning Guide

LESSON 9

Scales

The word **scale** comes from the Latin word *scala*, which means "ladder." There are many different musical scales. The first scale we will learn is called the **major scale**.

Singing the C Major Scale, Ascending

Scales are named by the note they start on. This scale begins on C, so it is called the C major scale.

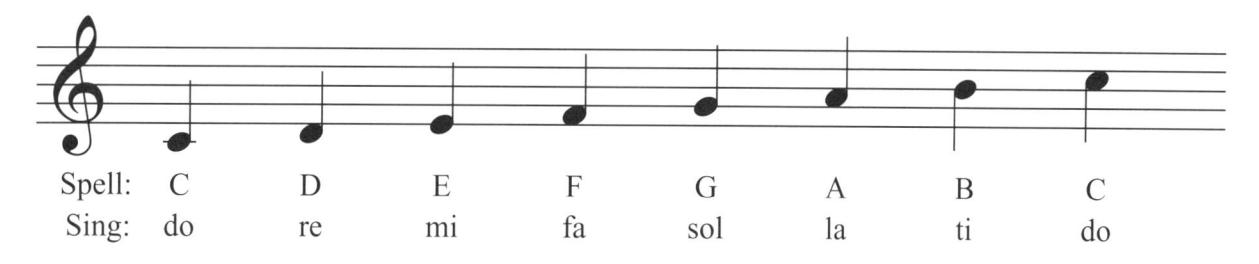

Spell: C   D   E   F   G   A   B   C
Sing: do re mi fa sol la ti do

On the staff, when notes go up in pitch, we say they are **ascending**. The scale above is an ascending C major scale. You can sing the notes of the scale using letter names (A, B, C) or pitch syllables (do, re, mi).

Intervals

An **interval** is the distance between two notes.

To determine the size of an interval, count the total number of lines and spaces for the two notes. Count the line or space of the first note as "1." *Make sure you include the lines or spaces of both notes in your total.*

Another way to find the size of an interval is to spell the letter names between the two notes. The total number of letter names is the size of the interval. Remember to include both notes of the interval in your total.

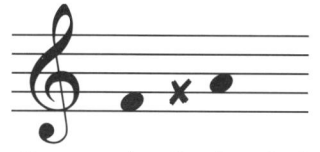

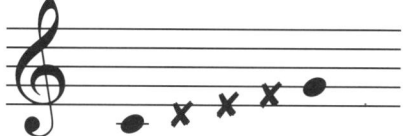

Count: 1 2 3 = 3rd   Count: 1 2 3 4 5 = 5th   Count: 1 2 3 4 5 6 7 = 7th
Spell: F G A   Spell: C D E F G   Spell: E F G A B C D

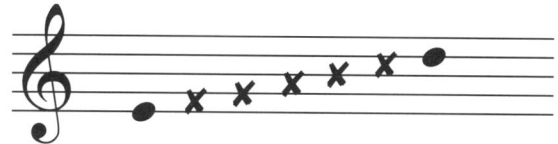

Sound Advice Level 1   Lesson 9 Learning Guide   43

LESSON 9 Learning Guide

2nds (Steps)

Moving from left to right on a keyboard, the white keys move up by step in the same order as the music alphabet. The distance from one white key to the very next white key is a **2nd**. Sometimes 2nds are called **steps**.

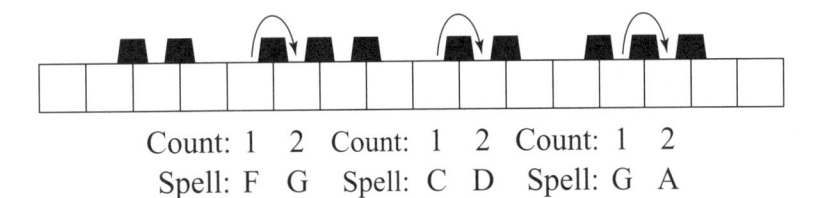

Count: 1 2   Count: 1 2   Count: 1 2
Spell: F G   Spell: C D   Spell: G A

When notes move from a line to the nearest space, *or* from a space to the nearest line, they are moving by 2nds. Count the low note as "1" and the note a step up as "2." When you spell a 2nd, start with one note in the music alphabet and move to the very next one.

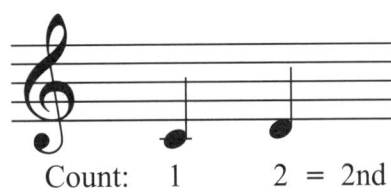

Count: 1   2 = 2nd   Count: 1   2 = 2nd   Count: 1   2 = 2nd
Spell: F   G   Spell: C   D   Spell: G   A

44 Lesson 9 Learning Guide Sound Advice Level 1

Theory Worksheet

LESSON 9

1 Draw four treble clefs and four bass clefs on the staff below.

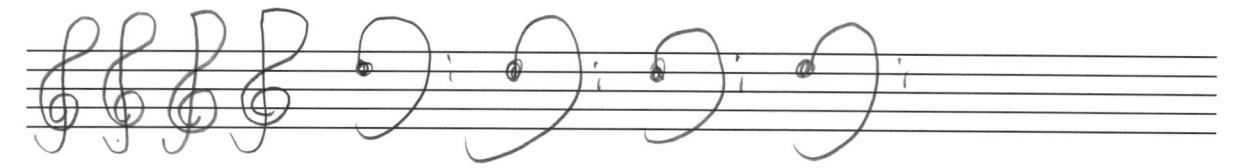

2 Spell the note that is a 2nd *above* these note names.

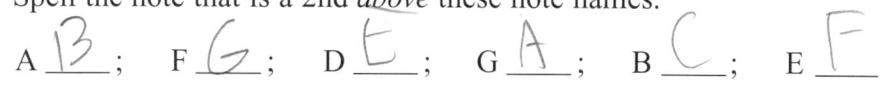

A _B_ ; F _G_ ; D _E_ ; G _A_ ; B _C_ ; E _F_

3 Spell the note that is a 2nd *below* these note names.

B _A_ ; D _C_ ; G _F_ ; C _B_ ; E _D_ ; A _G_

4 Draw an arrow from each note marked ✘ to the note that is a 2nd *above*. The first arrow has been drawn for you.

5 Write a note that is a 2nd *above* each of these notes. Name both notes.

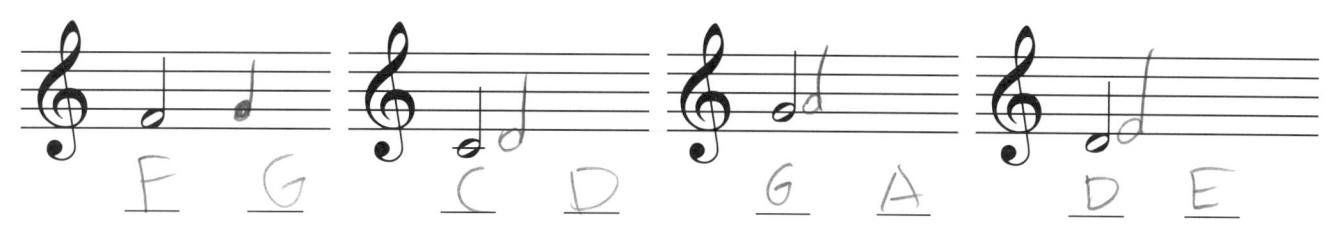

F G ; C D ; G A ; D E

6 Name the size of the following intervals.

3rd ; 2nd ; 7th ; 5th

7 Rhythm Jumble: Record the number of days you practiced.

Sound Advice Level 1 — Lesson 9 Theory Worksheet — 45

LESSON 9 Ear-Training Worksheet

Track 41

1 **Sight Singing:**

a) Pause the recording. Sing the following ascending C major scale.

b) Turn to the answer key and sing along with the recording.

Track 42

2 **Error Detection:** Circle any notes in the following major scale that are not played correctly.

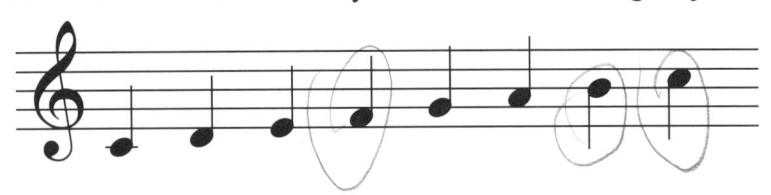

Track 43

3 **Melodic Identification:** Identify the correct notation for the melody you hear.

a)

b)

Track 44

4 **Sight Singing:**

a) Pause the recording. Sing the following melody while you tap a steady quarter-note beat.

b) Turn to the answer key and sing along with the recording.

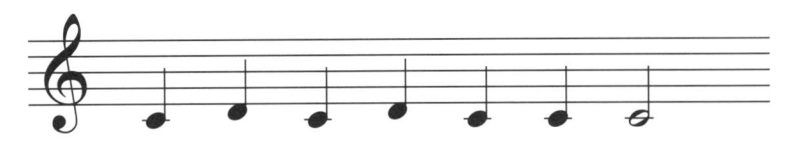

Track 45

5 **Melodic Dictation:**

Sing back the melody you hear from memory. Listen to the recording as many times as you need. Then write the melody on the staff below. The melody begins on Middle C.

I LISTENED ☐ TIMES

Sing it first, then write it down.

46   Lesson 9 Ear-Training Worksheet   Sound Advice Level 1

Learning Guide

LESSON 10

3rds (Skips)

On the white keys of a keyboard, you can move a 3rd by skipping a key. This is why 3rds are sometimes called "skips." You can also find a 3rd by counting three white keys.

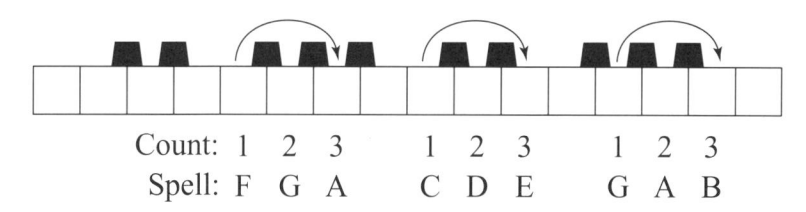

Count: 1 2 3   1 2 3   1 2 3
Spell: F G A   C D E   G A B

On the staff, the notes of a 3rd move from "line to line" or "space to space." Count the lower note as "1," the skipped note as "2," and the next note as "3." When you spell 3rds, skip one letter name. Study the examples below.

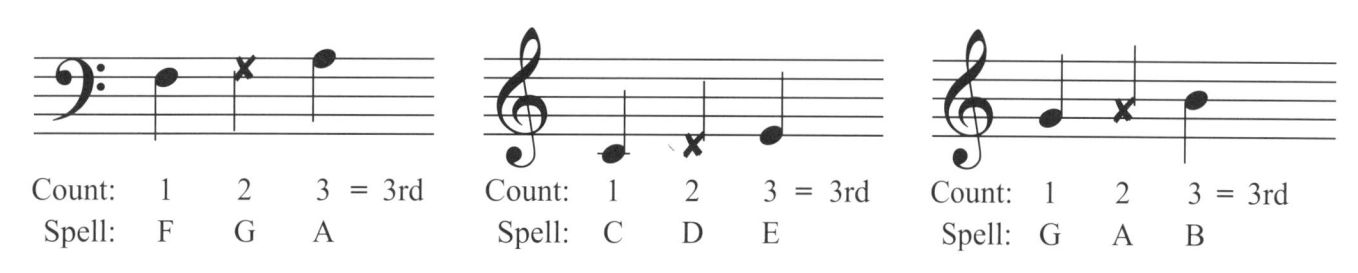

Count: 1 2 3 = 3rd   Count: 1 2 3 = 3rd   Count: 1 2 3 = 3rd
Spell: F G A   Spell: C D E   Spell: G A B

Singing the C Major Scale, Ascending and Descending

In Lesson 9, you sang and played a C major scale **ascending** (going up). Now you can also sing and play this scale **descending** (going down). Sing or play this scale in both directions in your daily ear-training practice.

do re mi fa sol la ti do ti la sol fa mi re do

Sound Advice Level 1   Lesson 10 Learning Guide   47

LESSON 10 Theory Worksheet

1) This question has five steps. Complete each step before moving to the next.

a) Print the music alphabet, going up by step, as many times as you can in the spaces below.

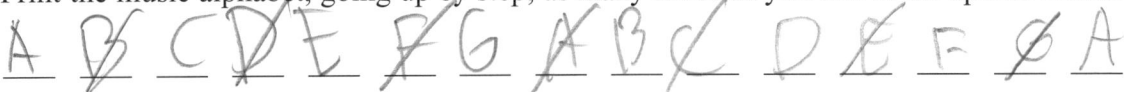

A B C D E F G A B C D E F G A

b) Cross out every other letter above, starting with **B**.

c) In the spaces below, write the letters that are *not* crossed out.

A C E G B D F A

d) The note names you just wrote move by 3rds (skips). Name these notes out loud until you can say them easily and quickly.

e) Name the notes on the grand staff below. Are they the same as the ones above?

(Treble clef notes): D F A
(Bass clef notes): A C E G B

2) Name the size of the following intervals. Choose 2nds or 3rds.

3rds — 2nds — 3rds — 2nds — 2nds

3) Draw a curved arrow from each note marked ✗ to the note that is a 3rd *above*. The first arrow has been drawn for you.

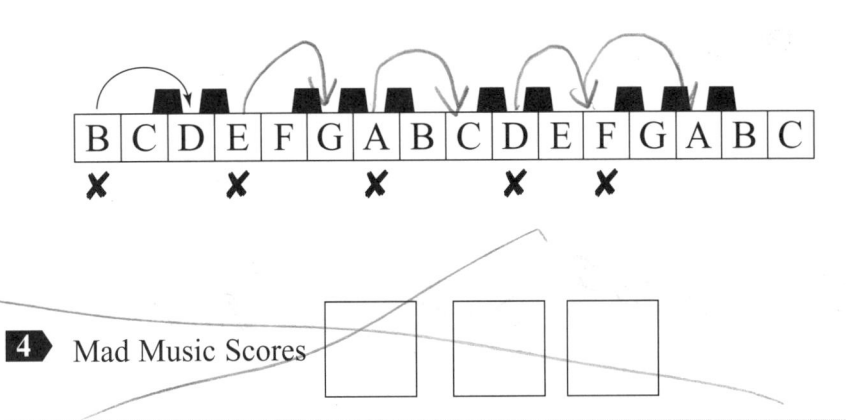

B C D E F G A B C D E F G A B C
✗   ✗   ✗   ✗ ✗

4) Mad Music Scores

Ear-Training Worksheet

LESSON 10

1) Sight Singing:
a) Pause the recording. Sing the following C major scale, ascending and descending.
b) Turn to the answer key and sing along with the recording.

2) Error Detection: Circle any notes in this major scale that are not played correctly.

3) Melodic Identification: Identify the correct notation for the melody you hear.

4) Sight Singing:
a) Pause the recording. Sing the following melody while you tap a steady quarter-note beat.
b) Turn to the answer key and sing along with the recording.

5) Melodic Dictation: Sing back the melody you hear from memory. Listen to the recording as many times as you need. Then write the melody on the staff below. The melody begins on Middle C.

6) Interval Identification: Identify the intervals you hear as 2nds or 3rds. Each interval will be played twice.

a) 2nds b) 3rds c) 2nds d) 2nds e) 3rds

Lesson 11 Learning Guide

Bar Lines and Measures

A **bar line** is a vertical line that separates one group of notes from the next. The space between two bar lines is called a **measure**.

A **double bar line** marks the end of a piece of music. In longer works, double bar lines can also mark the end of a section. The second line is twice as thick as the first.

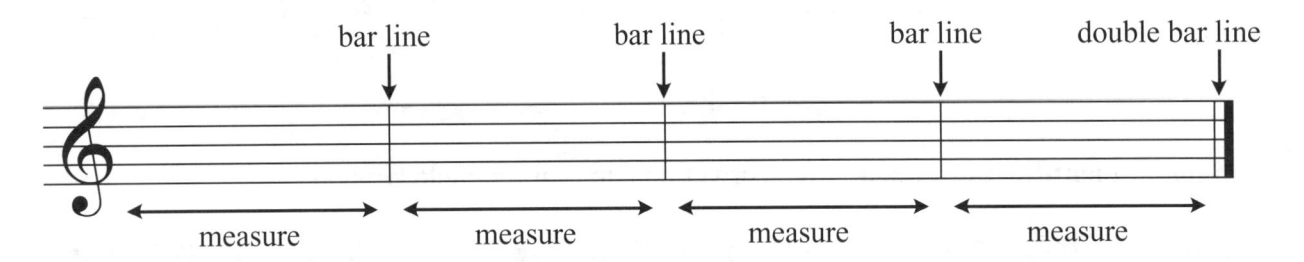

Meter

In most of the music you hear or play, some beats seem stronger—or more accented—than others. A repeating pattern of strong and weak beats is called **meter**.

Sing the two rhythmic patterns below. Feel the accented and non-accented notes as shown by the symbols ′ (strong) and ˘ (weak).

Example 1:

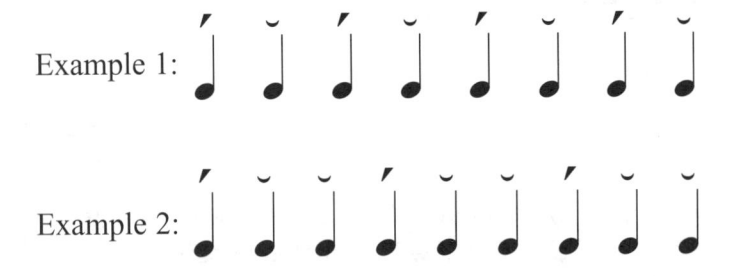

Example 2:

The pattern of strong and weak beats in these two examples is different. This means that Example 1 and Example 2 have different meters.

Duple Meter

When beats are grouped in a "strong-weak" pattern, as in Example 1 above, we call it **duple meter**. In duple meter, there are **two beats in each measure**. Study the example below.

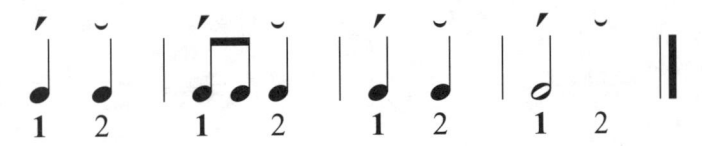

LESSON 11

Learning Guide

Time Signature $\frac{2}{4}$

We use a **time signature** to show the meter. A time signature has two numbers.
The top number tells you the number of beats in each measure.
The bottom number tells you what kind of note gets one beat.

$\frac{2}{4}$ = $\frac{2}{\quad}$ ← Number of beats
        ← Beat note (♩)

The melody below has a time signature of $\frac{2}{4}$. This means that there are two beats in each measure. The time signature only appears in the first measure of the first line of music.

Remember that the first beat of every measure is always the strong beat.

Measure Numbers

When you learn a piece of music, it is helpful to number the measures. If your teacher says "look at measure 12," you will know where to look. Count the *first complete* measure as measure 1.

In your own music, you can number each measure. In most published music, measure numbers are placed at the beginning of each line, and measure 1 is not labeled.

Allegro
op. 1, no. 1

Alexander Reinagle
(1756–1809)

When you number the measures in your own music, write the number directly over the first beat of the measure.

Sound Advice Level 1   Lesson 11 Learning Guide   51

LESSON 11 Theory Worksheet

1 Name the following notes.

G B D E F E D C A

2 Name the following notes.

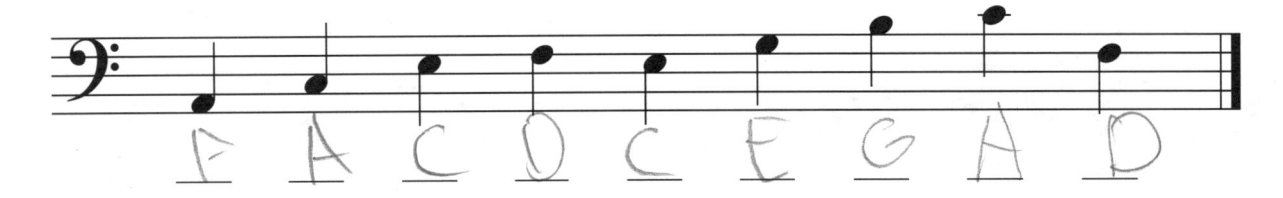

F A C D C E G A D

3 a) Write the symbols for strong (′) and weak (˘) beats over each measure to show the accent pattern.

b) Number the measures, then circle the third measure.

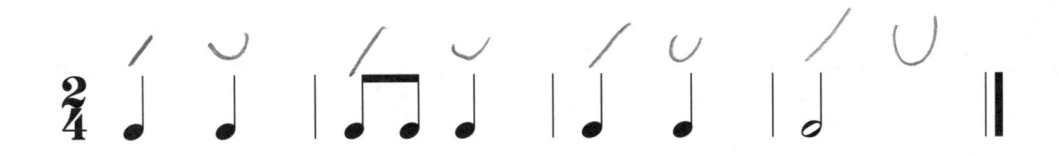

4 Circle the quarter-note beats, then add bar lines according to the time signature. To show that a half note is two quarter-note beats long, circle it (as shown), and write two quarter notes in the circle.

5 Rhythm Jumble: Record the number of days you practiced.

52   Lesson 11 Theory Worksheet   Sound Advice Level 1

Ear-Training Worksheet

Lesson 11

1. Rhythmic Identification: Identify the correct notation for the rhythmic pattern you hear.

a)
b)

2. Rhythmic Reading:
a) Pause the recording. Sing the following rhythmic pattern while you tap a steady quarter-note beat. Make sure you feel the accents for duple meter.
b) Turn to the answer key and sing along with the recording.

3. Rhythmic Dictation: Sing, tap, or clap the rhythmic pattern you hear from memory, then write it in the space below. The rhythm is in 2/4 time.

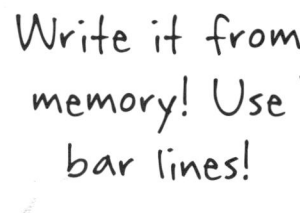

Write it from memory! Use bar lines!

4. Sight Singing:
a) Pause the recording. Sing the following melody while you tap a steady quarter-note beat.
b) Turn to the answer key and sing along with the recording.

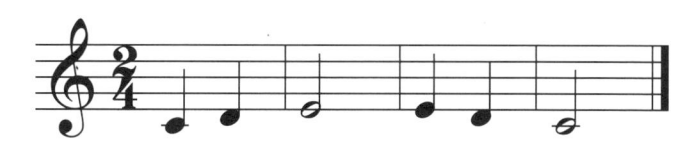

5. Interval Identification: Identify the intervals you hear as 2nds or 3rds.

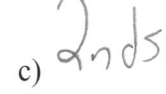

a) 3rds   b) 2nds   c) 2nds   d) 3rds   e) 2nds

Sound Advice Level 1 — Lesson 11 Ear-Training Worksheet — 53

Lesson 12

Learning Guide

Ties

A tie joins two notes together into one continuous sound. The length of the sound is equal to the total length of the two notes.

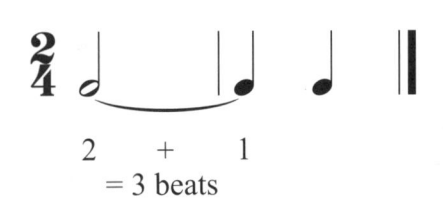

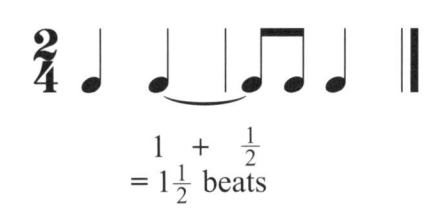

$$2 + 1 = 3 \text{ beats}$$

$$1 + \tfrac{1}{2} = 1\tfrac{1}{2} \text{ beats}$$

New Rhythmic Unit

This new rhythmic unit consists of a quarter note tied to the first of two eighth notes:

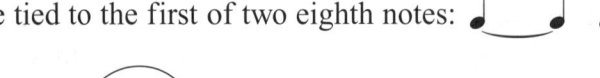

This unit equals two quarter-note beats:

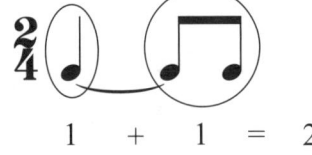

$$1 + 1 = 2$$

Look at the two examples below, then sing them. In Example 2, carry the sound of the tied quarter notes *through* the eighth notes to which they are tied. Tap your finger as you sing.

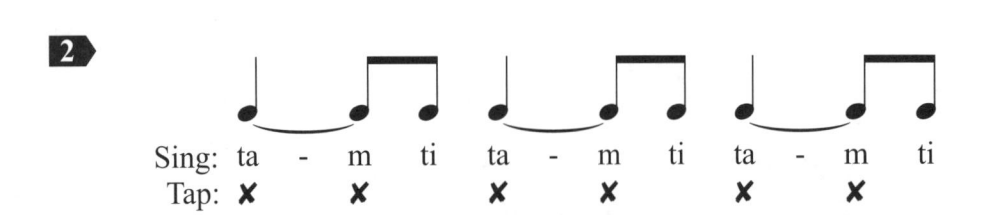

1

Sing: ta ti ti ta ti ti ta ti ti
Tap: ✗ ✗ ✗ ✗ ✗ ✗

2

Sing: ta - m ti ta - m ti ta - m ti
Tap: ✗ ✗ ✗ ✗ ✗ ✗

Learning Guide

LESSON 12

Tap your finger while you sing the patterns below, following the arrows. Notice that your finger touches the surface once for each quarter-note beat.

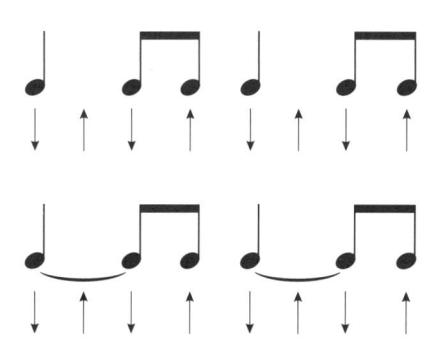

Each arrow measures half a beat!

Circle this new rhythmic unit on the Rhythm Jumble Chart (see p. 115).

Rhythm Jumble Games

Since Lesson 8 you have been recording the number of times you used the Rhythm Jumble Chart to sight-read rhythms. Now you are ready to play one of the three Rhythm Jumble Games described on p. 116.

1) Rhythm Jumble Reading
2) Rhythm Jumble Solitaire
3) Rhythm Jumble Composer

You and your teacher can decide which game is best for you. Play a Rhythm Jumble Game at least three times before your next lesson. Write your scores in the boxes on your Theory Worksheet.

Sound Advice Level 1 — Lesson 12 Learning Guide

LESSON 12 Theory Worksheet

1 Circle the quarter-note beats, then add bar lines according to the time signature. Identify the strong and weak beats by writing the ′ (strong) and ⌣ (weak) symbols above the notes.

2 Circle the quarter-note beats, then add a time signature.

3 Identify the following intervals as 2nds or 3rds.

2nds   3rds   2nds   3rds

4 Draw a bass clef at the beginning of the staff, then name the notes.

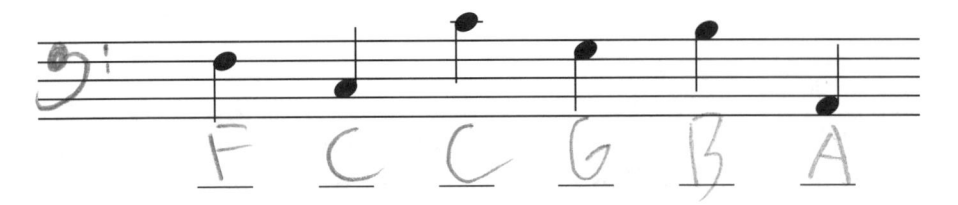

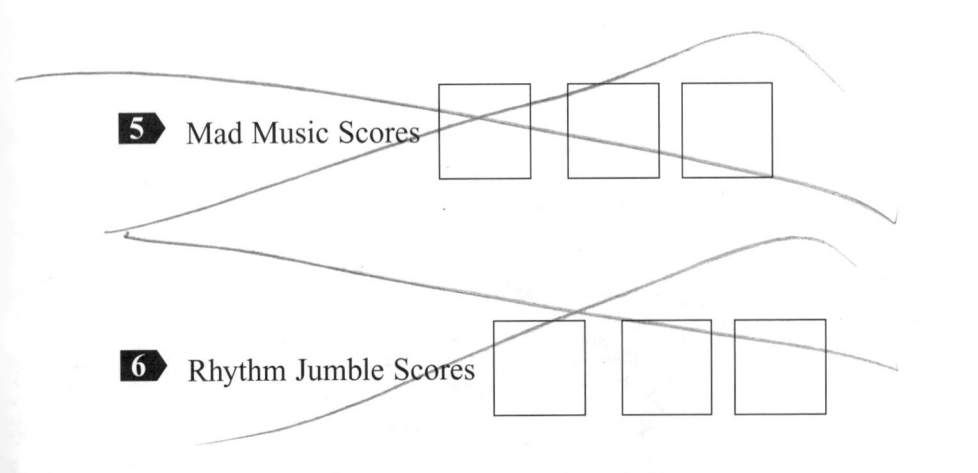

F C C G B A

5 Mad Music Scores

6 Rhythm Jumble Scores

Ear-Training Worksheet

LESSON 12

Track 57

1) Rhythmic Reading:

a) Pause the recording. Sing the following rhythmic pattern while you tap a steady quarter-note beat.

b) Turn to the answer key and sing along with the recording.

Track 58

2) Rhythmic Reading:

a) Pause the recording. Sing the following rhythmic pattern while you tap a steady quarter-note beat.

b) Turn to the answer key and sing along with the recording.

Track 59

3) Editing:

a) Add ties where you hear them in the following rhythmic pattern. Listen to the example as many times as you need.

b) Sing the edited rhythmic pattern while you tap a steady quarter-note beat.

Track 60

4) Rhythm Singback/Clapback: Sing, tap, or clap the rhythmic pattern you hear from memory. Listen to the example as many times as you need.

I LISTENED ___ TIMES

Track 61

5) Interval Identification: The first note of each interval is given below. Name the interval you hear as a 2nd or a 3rd, then write the second note. Each interval will be played twice.

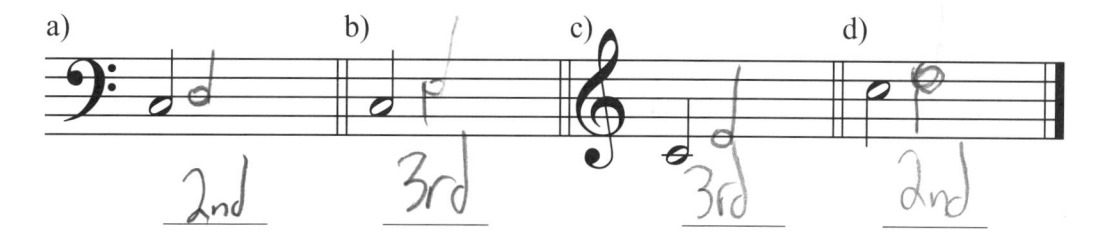

a) 2nd   b) 3rd   c) 3rd   d) 2nd

Sound Advice Level 1   Lesson 12 Ear-Training Worksheet   57

Lesson 13 Learning Guide

The Quarter Rest 𝄽

Rests are symbols for silence. A **quarter rest** is the symbol for one quarter-note beat of silence. When you sing a rhythm that has a quarter rest, you can say *sh* or just *be silent* on the rests.

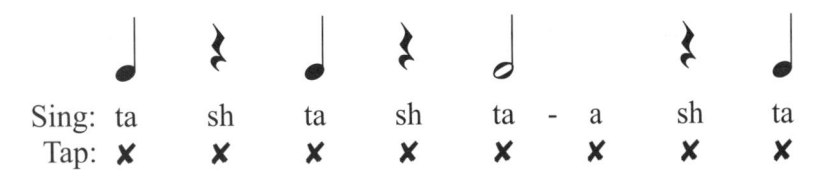

𝄽 = ♩

| Sing: | ta | sh | ta | sh | ta - a | sh | ta |
| Tap: | x | x | x | x | x x | x | x |

Turn to the Rhythm Jumble Chart on p. 115 and circle the quarter rest. From now on, you can include the quarter rest when you play Rhythm Jumble.

How to Draw a Quarter Rest

1 Draw a "lightening bolt" in spaces 4, and 3, and 2:

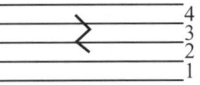

2 Add a half circle in spaces 2 and 1:

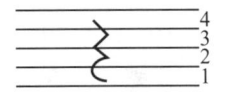

Naming Intervals

The full name of an interval tells you two things: size and quality. The **size** is shown with a number. The **quality** is shown by a word—or an abbreviation—that describes the interval's unique sound.

Here are all the intervals that you can write above C using only notes of the C major scale.

The 2nd, 3rd, 6th, and 7th are **major intervals** (maj). The quality of these four intervals is always major if the upper note belongs to the major scale.

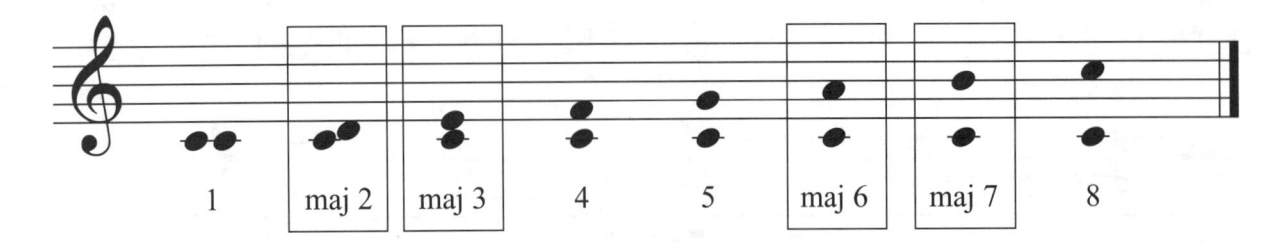

| 1 | maj 2 | maj 3 | 4 | 5 | maj 6 | maj 7 | 8 |

58   Lesson 13 Learning Guide   Sound Advice Level 1

Learning Guide

LESSON 13

The 2nds and 3rds shown below are all built on a C. They are major intervals because the upper notes (D and E) belong to the same major scale as the lower note—in this case, the C major scale.

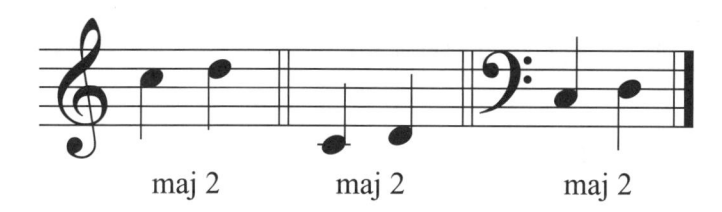

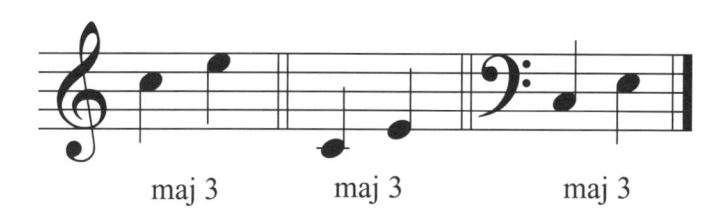

maj 2   maj 2   maj 2

maj 3   maj 3   maj 3

Later, we will build intervals using upper notes that do *not* belong to the major scale. When we do this, the sound—and the name—of the intervals will change.

The Sound of Major 2nds and Major 3rds

From now on, the interval identification questions in your Ear-Training Worksheets will include major 2nds and major 3rds. To learn the sound of these intervals, sing the following examples. Use pitch syllables or numbers:

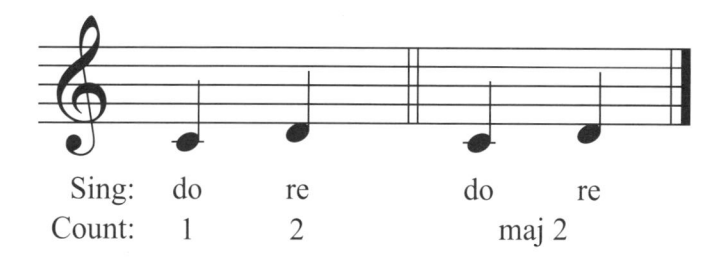

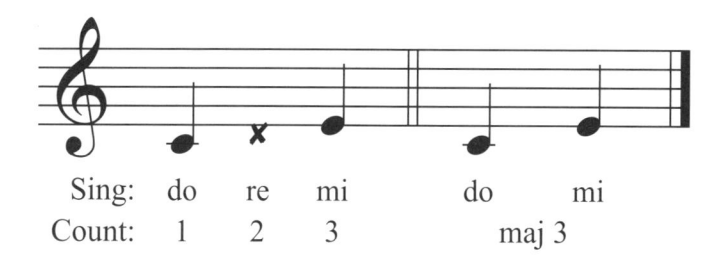

Sing: do   re   do   re
Count: 1   2   maj 2

Sing: do   re   mi   do   mi
Count: 1   2   3   maj 3

Place a ✔ beside the major 2nd and the major 3rd on your Song Clue Chart on p. 117.

Sound Advice Level 1   Lesson 13 Learning Guide   59

LESSON 13 — Theory Worksheet

1. Trace the quarter rest below, then draw five of your own. For extra practice, turn to the Drawing Symbols Chart on p. 114 and draw some more.

2. Name the following intervals as maj 2nds or maj 3rds.

maj 2   maj 3   maj 3   maj 2   maj 3   maj 2   maj 2

3. Circle the quarter-note beats. Add bar lines according to the time signature. Number the measures.

4. In the rhythmic pattern above, the first note in the third measure is a ___quarter note___ (half, quarter, eighth) note.

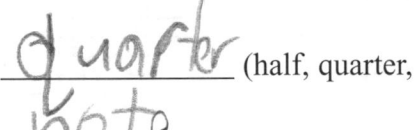

5. Rhythm Jumble Scores ☐ ☐ ☐

60   Lesson 13 Theory Worksheet   Sound Advice Level 1

Ear-Training Worksheet

LESSON 13

Track 62

1. Rhythmic Reading:

a) Pause the recording. Sing the following rhythmic pattern while you tap a steady quarter-note beat.

b) Turn to the answer key and sing along with the recording.

Track 63

2. Rhythmic Reading:

a) Pause the recording. Sing the following rhythmic pattern while you tap a steady quarter-note beat.

b) Turn to the answer key and sing along with the recording.

Track 64

3. Rhythm Clapback: Clap the *rhythm* of the melody you hear from memory. Record the number of times you listened.

I LISTENED 1 TIMES

Track 65

4. Sight Singing:

a) Pause the recording. Sing the following melodies while you tap a steady quarter-note beat.

b) Turn to the answer key and sing along with the recording.

Melody 1

Melody 2

Track 66

5. Melodic Identification: Identify the correct notation for the melody you hear.

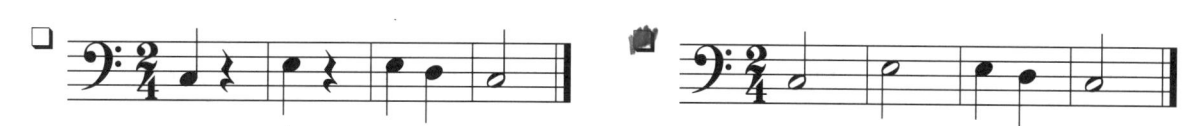

Track 67

6. Interval Identification: Identify the intervals you hear as maj 2nds or maj 3rds.

a) maj. 2nds b) maj. 3rds c) maj. 2nds d) maj. 2nds e) maj. 3rds

Remember to use your Song Clue Chart!

Sound Advice Level 1 — Lesson 13 Ear-Training Worksheet

Lesson 14 Learning Guide

5ths

You can find 5ths on a keyboard by counting five white keys in order. Count the first key as "1."

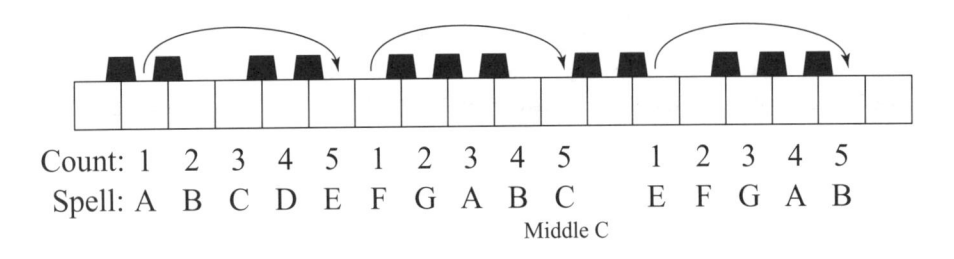

Count: 1 2 3 4 5 1 2 3 4 5 1 2 3 4 5
Spell: A B C D E F G A B C E F G A B
                                 Middle C

To find a 5th on the staff, count five lines and spaces from the first note. Make sure you count the first note as "1." You can also spell five letter names starting from the first note.

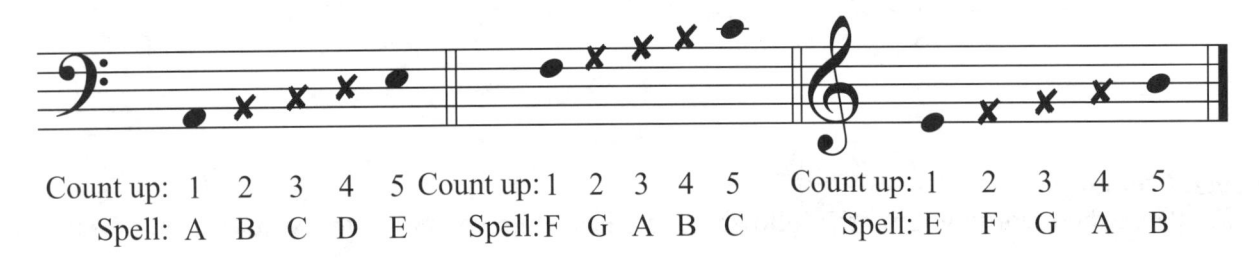

Count up: 1 2 3 4 5 Count up: 1 2 3 4 5 Count up: 1 2 3 4 5
Spell: A B C D E   Spell: F G A B C   Spell: E F G A B

Perfect Intervals

In Lesson 13, we learned that intervals are identified by their **size** (a number) and their **quality** (a word describing their unique sound). We looked at all the intervals that you can write above C using notes from the major scale. We also learned that 2nds, 3rds, 6ths, and 7ths are **major intervals** when the upper notes come from the major scale that begins on the bottom note.

All the other intervals—unison (U), 4th, 5th, and octave (8ve)—are called **perfect intervals** (P). In the example below, the lower note of each interval is C and the upper notes all belong to the C major scale.

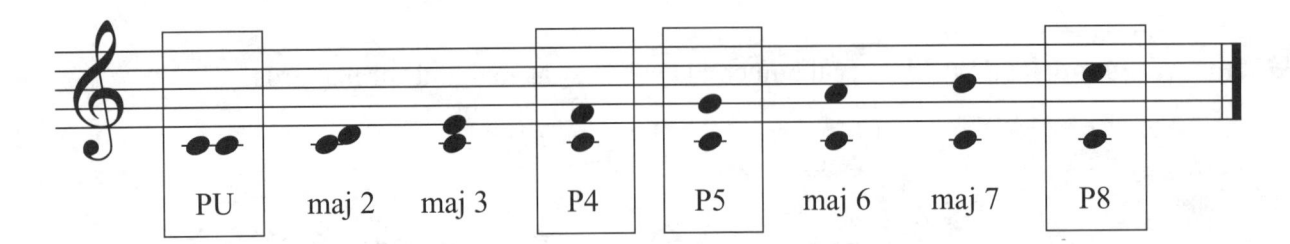

PU   maj 2   maj 3   P4   P5   maj 6   maj 7   P8

Learning Guide

LESSON 14

Memorize my license number! It lists all the perfect intervals!

PU458

The 5ths shown below are all built above a C. They are all **perfect 5ths** (P5) because the upper note (G) belongs to the same major scale as the lower note—in this case, the C major scale.

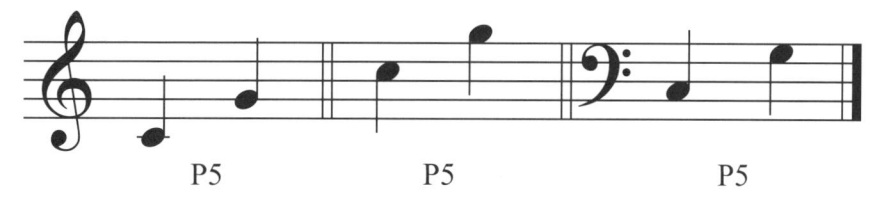

P5   P5   P5

The Sound of the Perfect 5th

From now on, the interval identification questions in your Ear-Training Worksheets will include perfect 5ths. To learn the sound of this interval, sing the following examples. Use syllables or numbers.

Sing: do re mi fa sol   do sol
Count: 1   2   3   4   5   P5

Place a ✔ beside the perfect 5th on your Song Clue Chart on p. 117.

Sound Advice Level 1   Lesson 14 Learning Guide   63

LESSON 14 Theory Worksheet

1 a) Draw a curved arrow from each note marked ✘ to the note a 5th *above*.
  b) Fill in the blanks in the chart below.

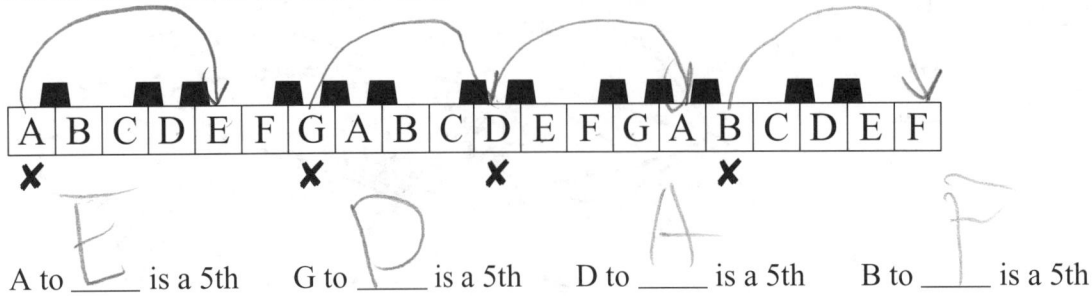

A to _E_ is a 5th   G to _D_ is a 5th   D to _A_ is a 5th   B to _F_ is a 5th

2 Name the size and quality of the following intervals.

P5ths   P4rth   maj.2nds   P5ths   maj.3rds

3 Write the following intervals above the given notes.

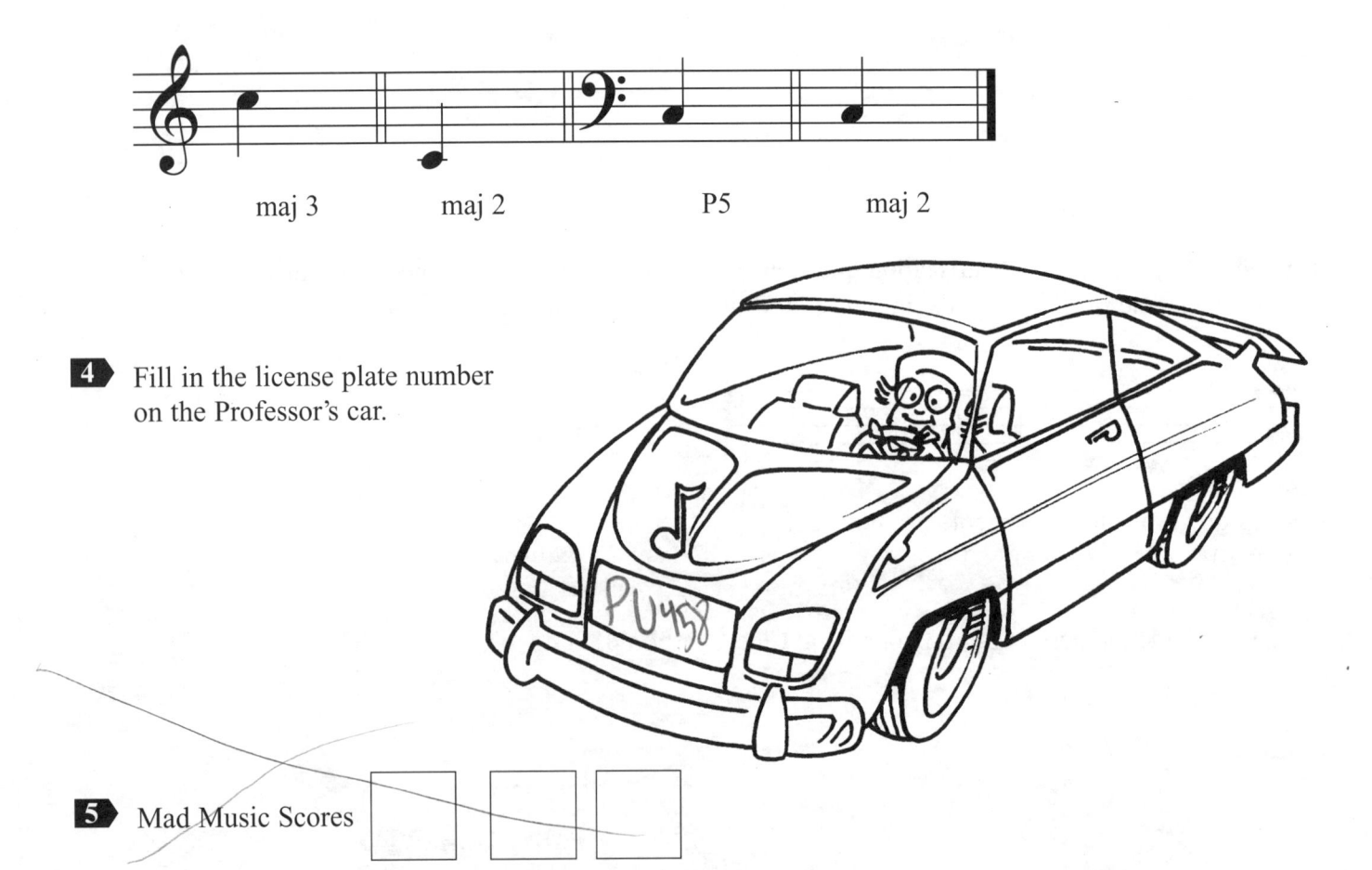

maj 3   maj 2   P5   maj 2

4 Fill in the license plate number on the Professor's car.

PU458

5 Mad Music Scores

Ear-Training Worksheet

1) Sight Singing:
   a) Pause the recording. Sing the C major scale, ascending and descending.
   b) Turn to the answer key and sing along with the recording.

2) Sight Singing:
   a) Pause the recording. Sing the following melody while you tap a steady quarter-note beat.
   b) Turn to the answer key and sing along with the recording.

3) Interval Identification: Identify the intervals you hear as maj 2, maj 3, or P5.

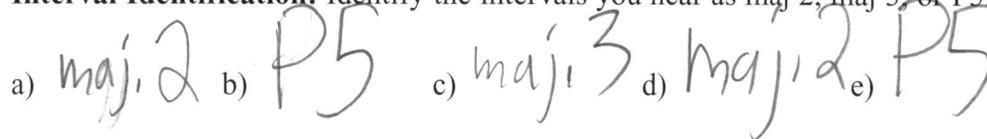

a) maj 2   b) P5   c) maj 3   d) maj 2   e) P5

4) Interval Identification: The first note of each interval is given. Name the interval you hear as a maj 2, maj 3, or P5, then write the second note.

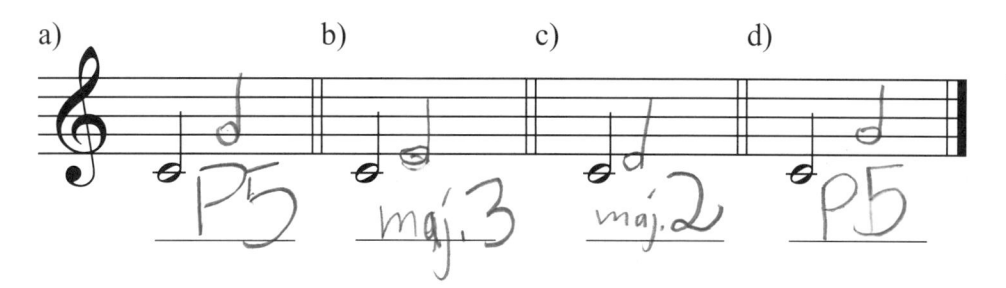

a) P5   b) maj 3   c) maj 2   d) P5

5) Editing:
   a) Add ties where you hear them in the following rhythmic pattern. Listen to the example as many times as you need.
   b) Sing the edited rhythmic pattern while you tap a steady quarter-note beat.

Add Ties!

Sound Advice Level 1 — Lesson 14 Ear-Training Worksheet — 65

Lesson 15 Learning Guide

The Dotted Half Note 𝅗𝅥.

This is a **dotted half note**: 𝅗𝅥.
The dot increases the length of the half note by half its value.

half note 𝅗𝅥 = 2 beats   half of 2 beats = 1 ♩   𝅗𝅥 + ♩ = 𝅗𝅥.
                                                    2 + 1 = 3 beats

Sing these dotted half notes while you tap a steady quarter-note beat.

𝅗𝅥.	𝅗𝅥.	𝅗𝅥.
Sing: ta - a - a	ta - a - a	ta - a - a
Tap: ✗ ✗ ✗	✗ ✗ ✗	✗ ✗ ✗

Triple Meter

When beats are grouped into a "strong-weak-weak" pattern, we call it **triple meter**. In triple meter, there are **three beats** in each measure.

New Time Signature 3/4

The top number of a time signature tells you the number of beats in each measure. The bottom number tells you what kind of note gets one beat.

3/4 = 3/♩   ← Number of beats
              ← Beat note (♩)

The rhythm below has a time signature of 3/4. This means that there are three beats in each measure.

1 2 3 | 1 2 3 | 1 2 3

Theory Worksheet — Lesson 15

1 Name the size and quality of the following intervals.

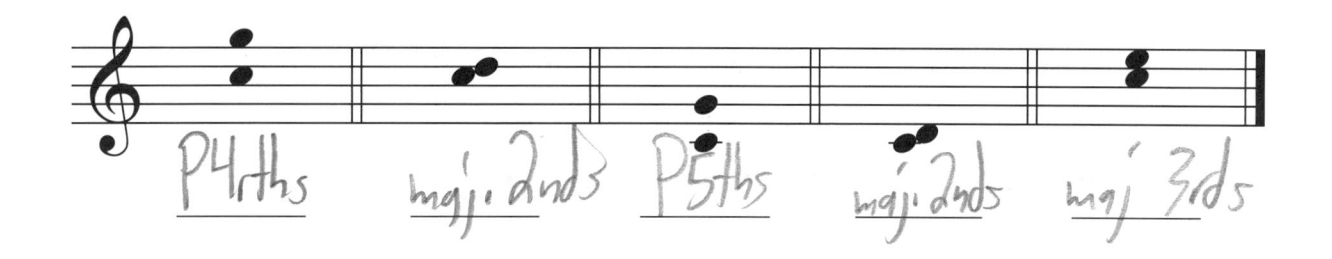

P4rths — maj. 2nds — P5ths — maj. 2nds — maj 3rds

2 Draw lines from each symbol in the center to its name and its number of beats.

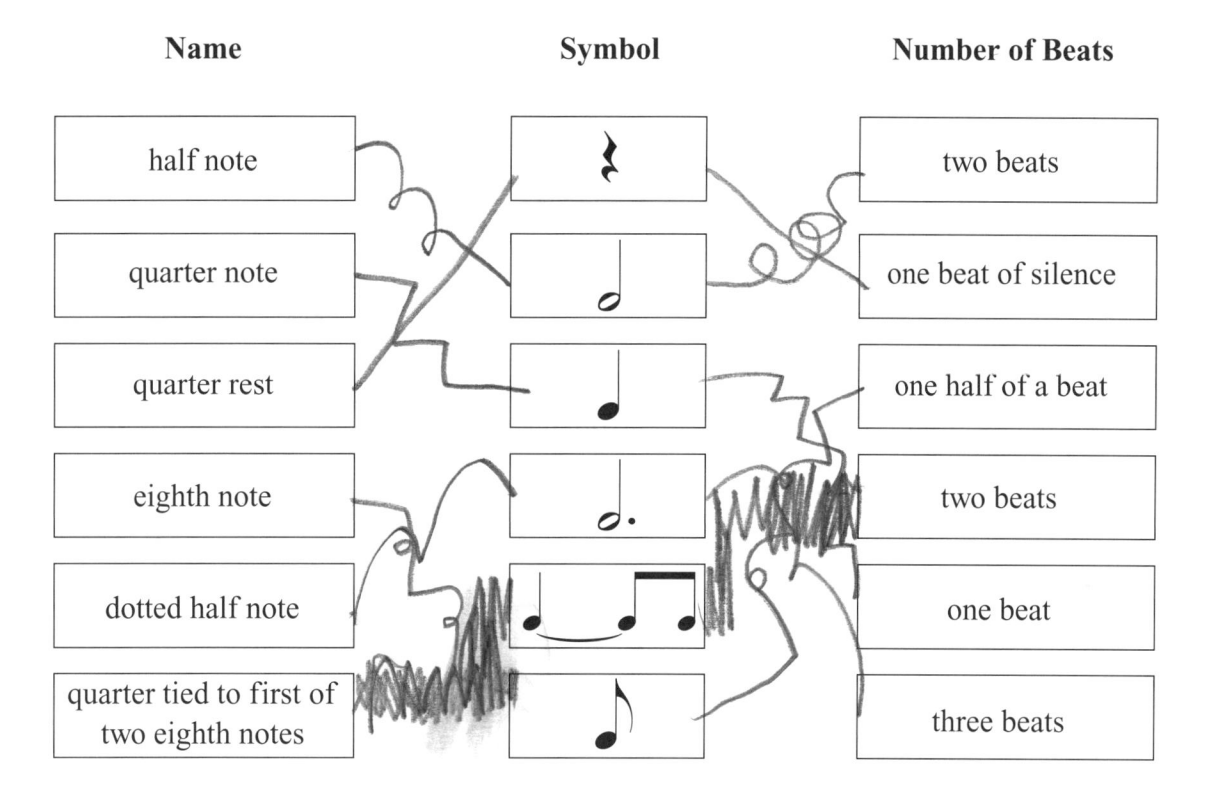

Name	Symbol	Number of Beats
half note	𝄽 (quarter rest)	two beats
quarter note	𝅗𝅥 (half note)	one beat of silence
quarter rest	𝅘𝅥 (quarter note)	one half of a beat
eighth note	𝅗𝅥. (dotted half)	two beats
dotted half note	two beamed eighths	one beat
quarter tied to first of two eighth notes	𝅘𝅥𝅮 (eighth note)	three beats

3 Circle the quarter-note beats. Add bar lines according to the time signature, then number the measures.

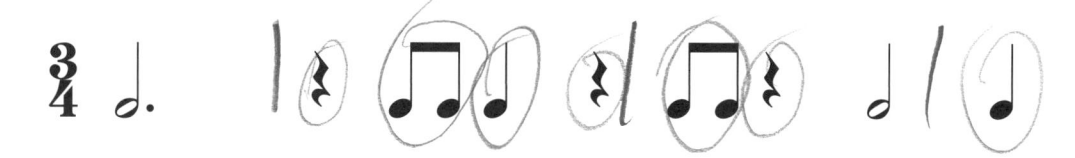

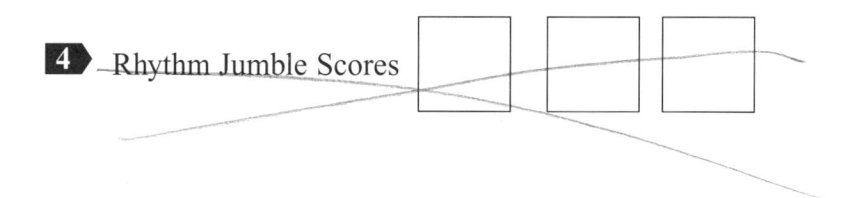

3/4

4 Rhythm Jumble Scores

LESSON 15

Ear-Training Worksheet

1. Rhythmic Reading:
 a) Pause the recording. Sing the following rhythmic pattern while you tap a steady quarter-note beat.
 b) Turn to the answer key and sing along with the recording.

2. Rhythm Clapback: Clap the *rhythm* of the melody you hear from memory. Record the number of times you listened.

I LISTENED 2 TIMES

3. Interval Identification: Identify the intervals you hear as maj 2, maj 3, or P5.
 a) P5   b) maj 3   c) maj 2   d) P5   e) maj 3

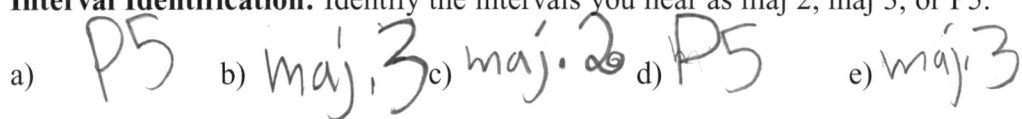

4. Sight Singing:
 a) Pause the recording. Sing the following melody while you tap a steady quarter-note beat.
 b) Turn to the answer key and sing along with the recording.

5. Melody Singback/Playback: Sing the melody you hear from memory, then play it back on your instrument. The melody begins on Middle C. Listen to the example as many times as you need. Record the number of times you listened.

I LISTENED 1 TIMES

6. Meter Identification: Identify the meter of the examples you hear as duple or triple. Tap a steady quarter-note beat as you listen.
 a) ☐ duple   b) ☑ duple
    ☑ triple   ☐ triple

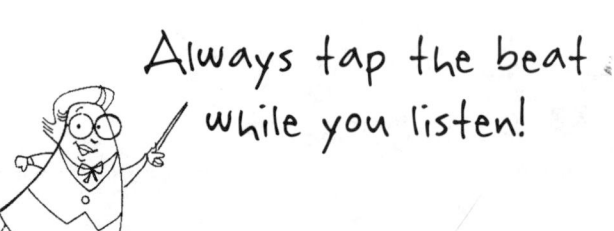

Always tap the beat while you listen!

Learning Guide

Lesson 16

4ths

You can find 4ths on a keyboard by counting four white keys. Count the first key as "1."

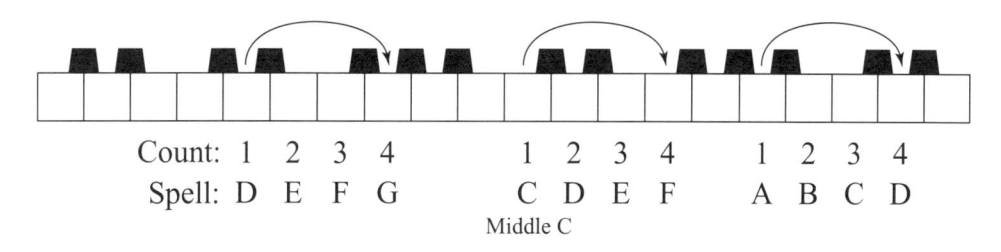

Count: 1 2 3 4   1 2 3 4   1 2 3 4
Spell: D E F G   C D E F   A B C D
                   Middle C

To find a 4th on the staff, count up four lines and spaces from the first note. Count the first note as "1." You can also spell four letter names starting from the first note.

Count up: 1 2 3 4   Count up: 1 2 3 4   Count up: 1 2 3 4
Spell: D E F G   Spell: C D E F   Spell: A B C D

The 4ths shown below are all built above a C. They are all **perfect 4ths** (P4) because the upper note (F) belongs to the same major scale as the lower note —in this case, the C major scale.

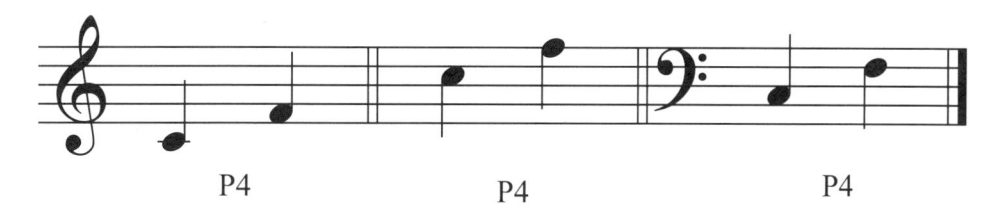

P4   P4   P4

Sound Advice Level 1   Lesson 16 Learning Guide

LESSON 16 Learning Guide

The Sound of the Perfect 4th

From now on, the interval identification questions in your Ear-Training Worksheets will include perfect 4ths. To learn the sound of this interval, sing the following examples. Use syllables or numbers.

Sing: do re mi fa do fa
Count: 1 2 3 4 P4

Place a ✔ beside the perfect 4th on your Song Clue Chart.

Interval Singing Drill

This drill will help you to memorize the sound of major 2nds, major 3rds, perfect 4ths, and perfect 5ths. Sing this drill every day. Here are three ways to sing it:

1 Sing the pitch syllables: do–re, do–mi, do–fa, do–sol, sol–fa–mi–re–do.

2 Sing the scale degree numbers: 1–2, 1–3, 1–4, 1–5, 5–4–3–2–1.

3 Sing the letter names: C–D, C–E, C–F, C–G, G–F–E–D–C.

Theory Worksheet

LESSON 16

1 a) Draw a curved arrow from each note marked ✘ to the note that is a 4th *above*.

b) Fill in the blanks in the chart below.

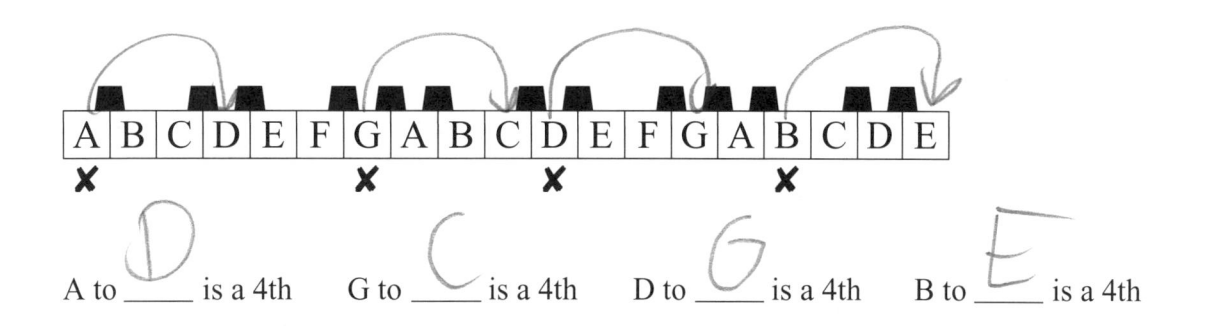

A to _D_ is a 4th   G to _C_ is a 4th   D to _G_ is a 4th   B to _E_ is a 4th

2 Name the following intervals.

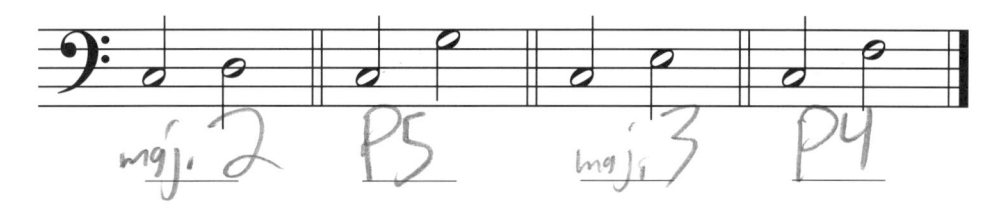

maj 2   P5   maj 3   P4

3 a) Sing or play the following melody.

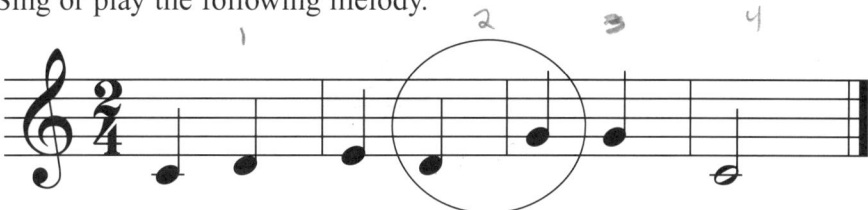

b) Number the measures.

c) Name the interval that is circled. _P4_

d) Name the note on the first beat of measure 2. _E_

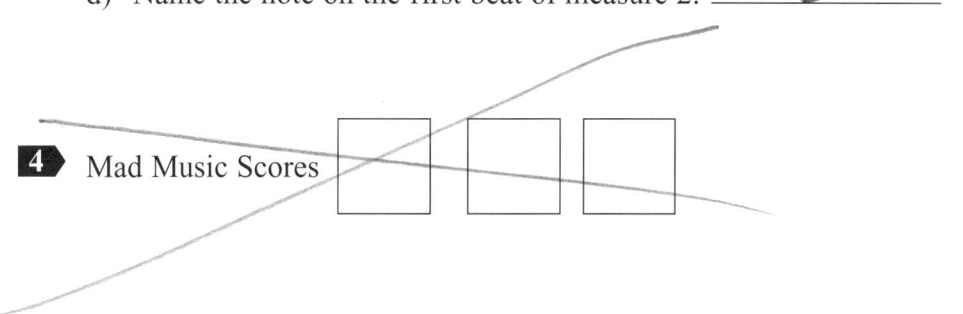

4 Mad Music Scores

Sound Advice Level 1 — Lesson 16 Theory Worksheet — 71

LESSON 16
Ear-Training Worksheet

1) Interval Identification: Identify the intervals you hear as maj 2, maj 3, P4, or P5.

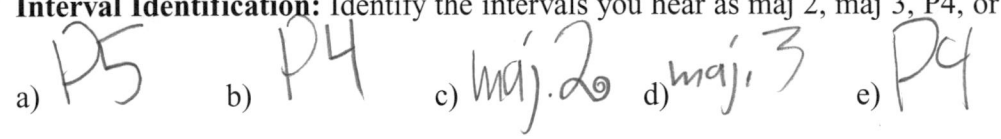

a) P5   b) P4   c) maj 2   d) maj 3   e) P4

2) Sight Singing:
a) Pause the recording. Sing the following melody while you tap a steady quarter-note beat.
b) Turn to the answer key and sing along with the recording.

3) Melody Singback/Playback: Sing the melody you hear from memory, then play it back on your instrument. The melody begins on Middle C.

I LISTENED [ ] TIMES

4) Rhythmic Dictation: Clap the *rhythm* of the melody you hear from memory, then write the rhythm in the space below. The rhythm is in 2/4 time.

I LISTENED [1] TIMES

5) Melodic Dictation: Sing back the melody you hear from memory, then write it on the staff below. The melody is in 3/4 time and begins on Middle C. Listen to the example as many times as you need.

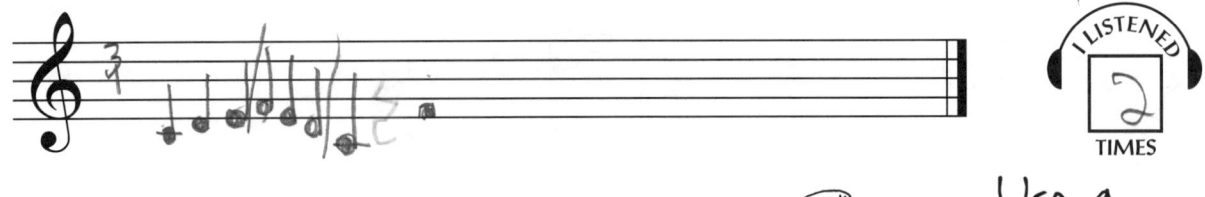

I LISTENED [2] TIMES

Use a time signature and bar lines!

Learning Guide

LESSON 17

Half Steps

A half step is the smallest interval you will learn.

On a piano keyboard, a half step is the distance from one key to the very next key, whether that key is black or white. Half steps are also called **semitones**.

On the neck of a guitar, the distance of a half step looks like this:

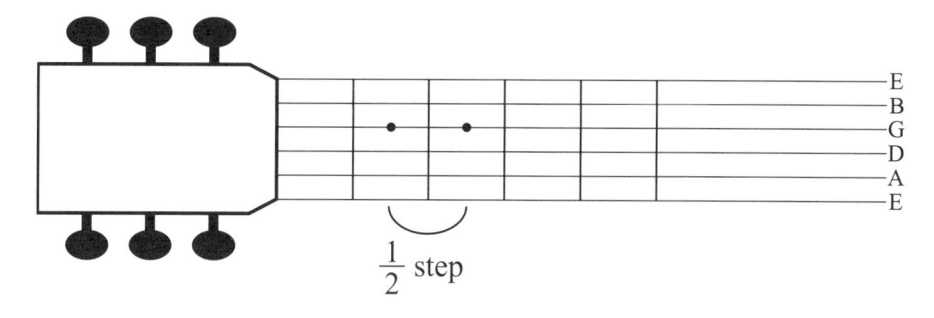

$\frac{1}{2}$ step

On the G string of a violin, the distance of a half step looks like this:

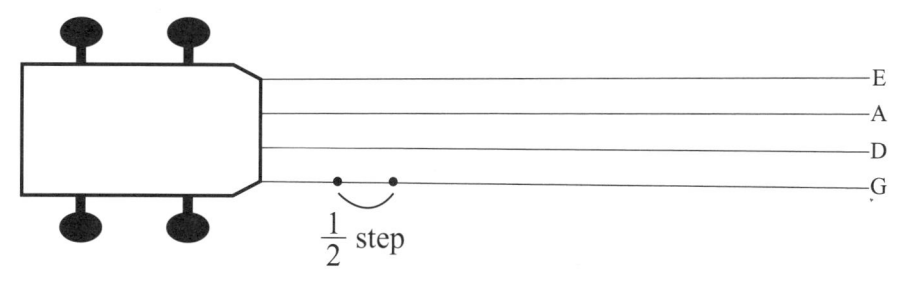

$\frac{1}{2}$ step

A half step is the same distance in sound on all instruments.

Sound Advice Level 1   Lesson 17 Learning Guide   73

LESSON 17 Learning Guide

White-Key Half Steps

On a piano keyboard, not all half steps involve a black key. The two half steps that use white keys are B to C and E to F.

White-key half steps:

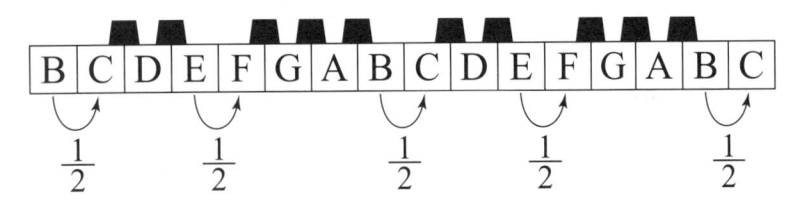

| B | C | D | E | F | G | A | B | C | D | E | F | G | A | B | C |

½ ½ ½ ½ ½

The Professor has a good way to remember the white-key half steps:

Bach Composed Every Friday

Accidentals: The Sharp Sign ♯

An **accidental** is a symbol that alters the pitch of a note.
The first accidental we will learn is the sharp sign.

The sharp sign in front of a note tells you to play the note a half step *higher*.
To remember this, think of what would happen if you sat on something *sharp* like a tack. You would jump *up!*

On a keyboard, *up* is the nearest key to the right. That key can be either black or white.
On a keyboard, B♯ is a white key that we normally call C, and E♯ is a white key that we normally call F.

| F | G | A | B | C | D | E | F |

F   F♯   B   B♯   E   E♯

Learning Guide

LESSON 17

How to Draw a Sharp Sign

1 The vertical lines of a sharp sign go straight up and down. Be careful not to draw them on an angle.

2 The sideways lines are on a slight angle, going *up* to the right.

3 Place the sharp *in front of* the note it raises. When you read music, you need to see the sharp before you play the note.

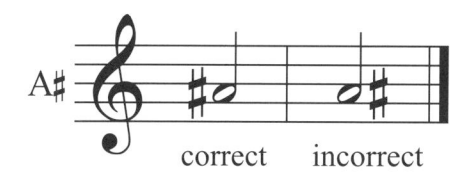

A# correct incorrect

4 Place the sharp on the *same line or space* as the notehead. If you cover the notehead, you should still be able to tell which note is raised.

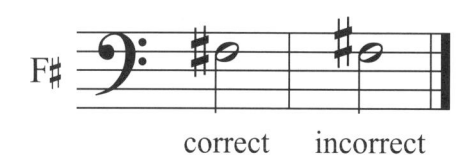

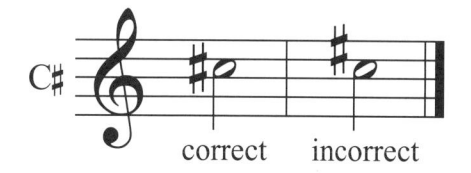

F# correct incorrect   C# correct incorrect

Sound Advice Level 1   Lesson 17 Learning Guide   75

LESSON 17 Theory Worksheet

1 Trace the sharp sign below, then draw four of your own. For extra practice, turn to the Drawing Symbols Chart on p. 114 and draw some more.

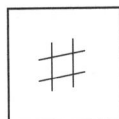

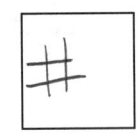

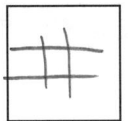

2 Draw a line from each note on the staff to its corresponding key on the keyboard. The first one has been done for you.

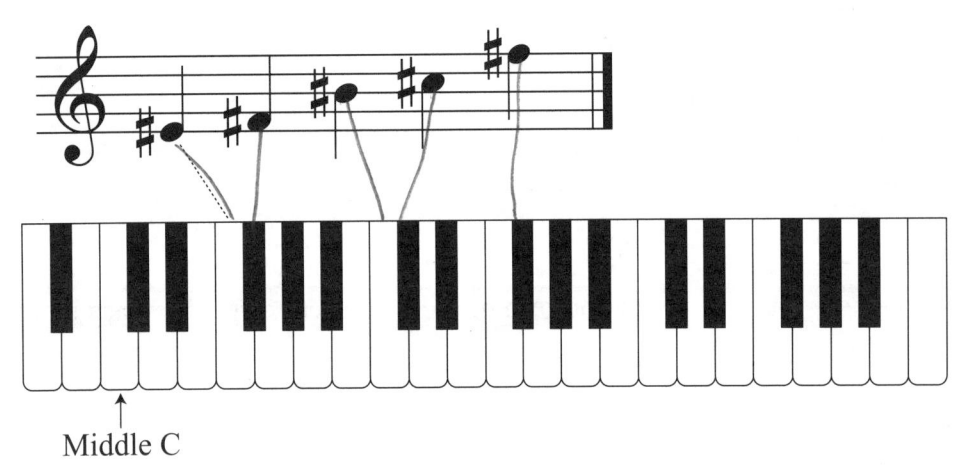

↑ Middle C

3 Name the following notes. Circle any pairs of notes that are a half step apart.

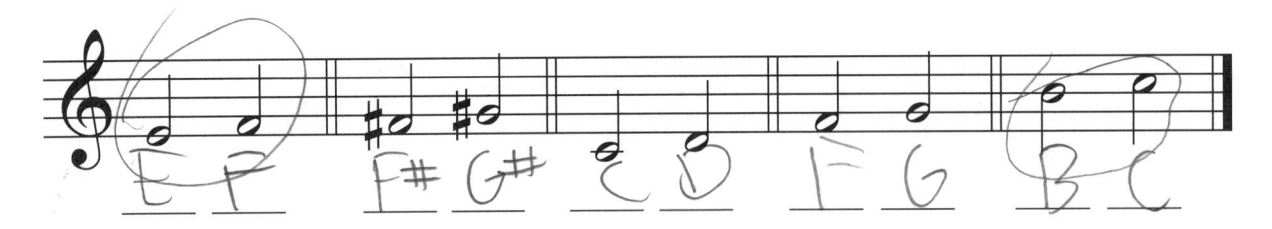

E F F# G# C D E G B C

4 Rhythm Jumble Scores

76   Lesson 17 Theory Worksheet   Sound Advice Level 1

Ear-Training Worksheet

Lesson 17

1. Interval Identification: Identify the intervals you hear as maj 2, maj 3, P4, or P5.

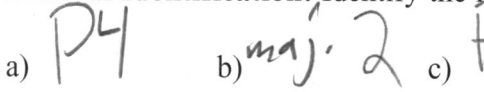

a) P4   b) maj 2   c) P5   d) maj 3   e) P4

2. Melody Singback/Playback: Sing the melody you hear from memory, then play it back on your instrument. The melody begins on Middle C.

3. Rhythmic Dictation: Clap the *rhythm* of the melody you hear from memory, then write the rhythm in the space below. The rhythm is in 3/4 time.

4. Error Detection: Circle any notes in the following melody that are not played correctly.

5. Editing: Listen to the following pairs of notes. The first note of each pair will be played as you see it below. Write a sharp in front of the *second* note if you hear the pitch go up a half step.

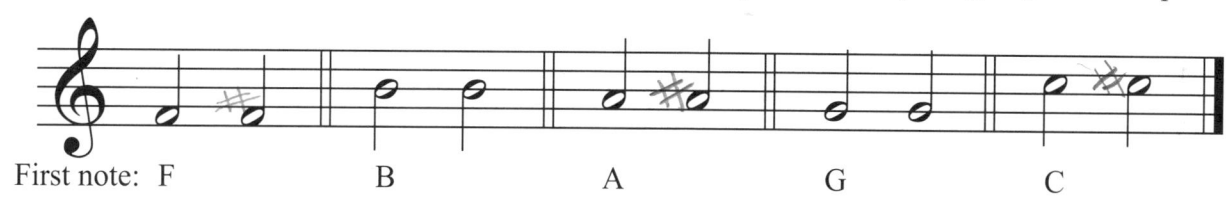

First note: F   B   A   G   C

Sound Advice Level 1   Lesson 17 Ear-Training Worksheet

Lesson 18 — Learning Guide

Accidentals: The Flat Sign ♭

The flat sign in front of a note tells you to play the note a half step *lower*. To remember this, think of what would happen if you were sitting in a car and all the tires went *flat*. You would go *down*!

On the keyboard, *down* is the nearest key to the left. That key can be either black or white.
On a keyboard, C♭ is a white key that we normally call B. F♭ is a white key that we normally call E.

How to Draw a Flat Sign

1 The vertical line of the flat sign goes straight up and down.

2 The curved line is like half of a heart (or a flattened circle).

3 Place the flat sign *in front of* the note it lowers.

4 Place the flat sign on the *same line or space* as the notehead. If you cover the notehead, you should still be able to see which note is lowered.

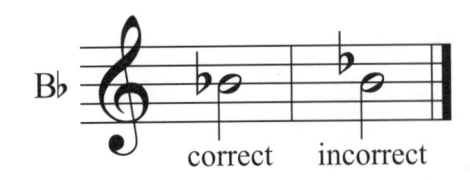

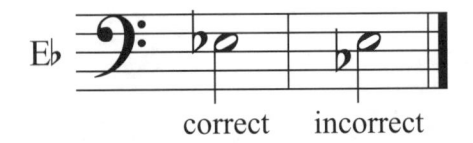

B♭   correct   incorrect   E♭   correct   incorrect

78   Lesson 18 Learning Guide   Sound Advice Level 1

Theory Worksheet

Lesson 18

1 Trace the flat sign below, then draw five of your own. For extra practice, turn to the Drawing Symbols Chart on p. 114 and draw some more.

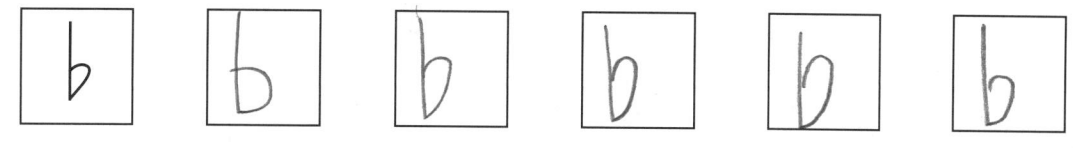

2 Draw a line from each note on the staff to its corresponding key on the keyboard.

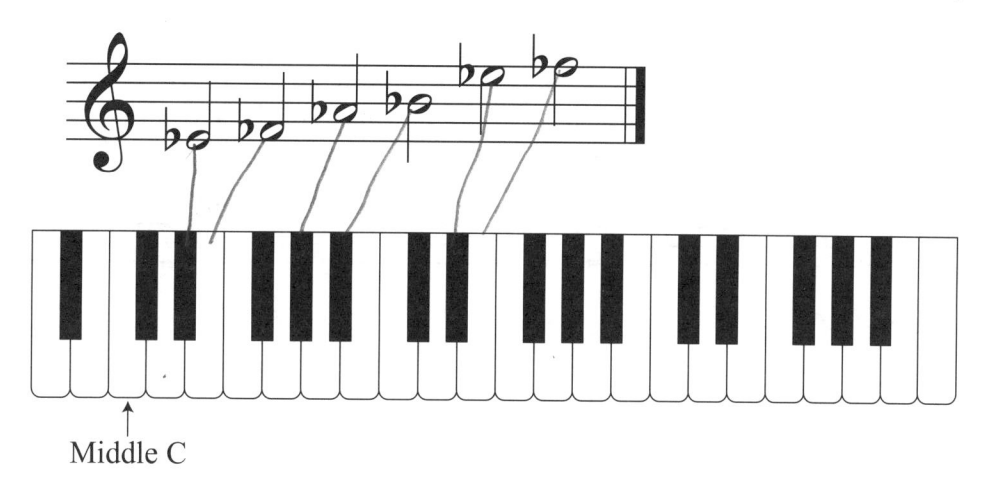

Middle C

3 Write accidentals in front of these notes as indicated. Draw lines from each note to its corresponding key on the keyboard.

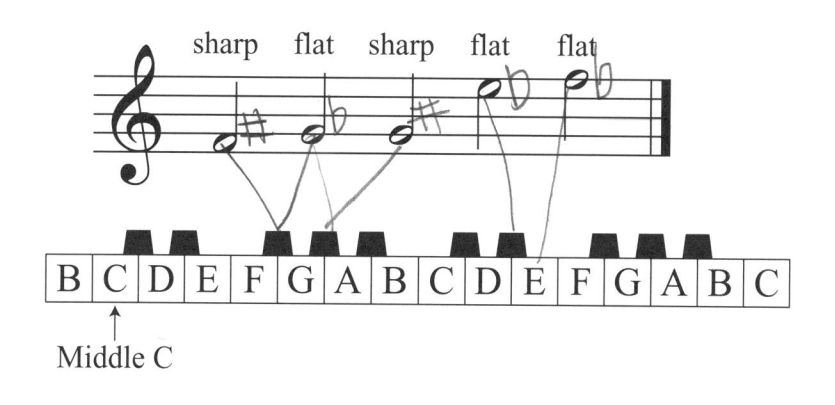

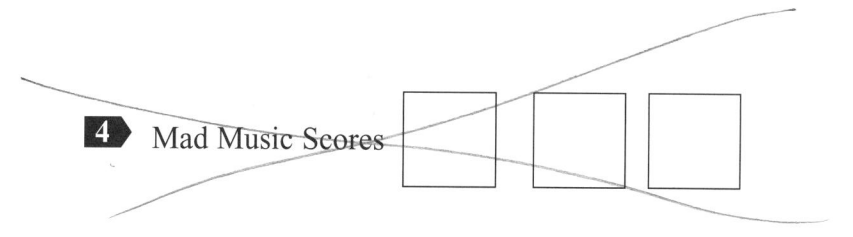

sharp   flat   sharp   flat   flat

| B | C | D | E | F | G | A | B | C | D | E | F | G | A | B | C |

Middle C

4 Mad Music Scores

Sound Advice Level 1 — Lesson 18 Theory Worksheet

LESSON 18

Ear-Training Worksheet

1. Interval Identification: The first note of each interval is given. Name the interval you hear, then write the second note.

a) b) c) d)

P4   P5   m2   P5

2. Editing: Listen to the following pairs of notes. The first note of each pair will be played as you see it below. Based on what you hear, write a sharp or a flat in front of the *second* note.

First note: F   C   D   G   A

3. Melodic Identification: Identify the correct notation for the melody you hear.

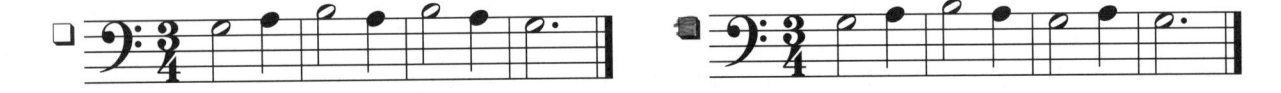

4. Rhythm Clapback: Clap the *rhythm* of the melody you hear from memory. Record the number of times you listened.

I LISTENED 1 TIMES

5. Melodic Dictation: Add the missing notes under the bracket. The melody will be played twice.

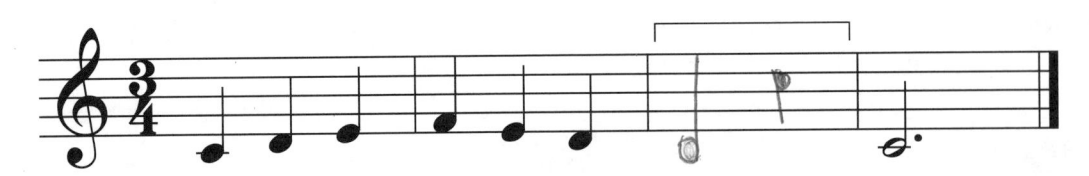

Learning Guide — Lesson 19

Whole Steps

On a piano keyboard, when you skip over *one* key (black or white), you move a **whole step**. Whole steps are also called **whole tones**.

| B | C | D | E | F | G | A | B | C |

On the neck of a guitar, the distance of a whole step looks like this:

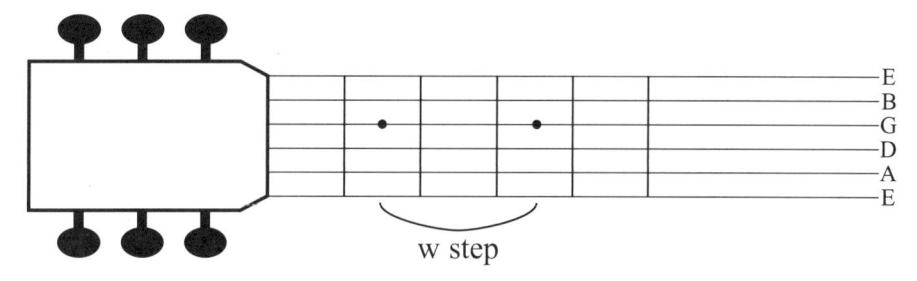

w step

E
B
G
D
A
E

On the G string of a violin, the distance of a whole step looks like this:

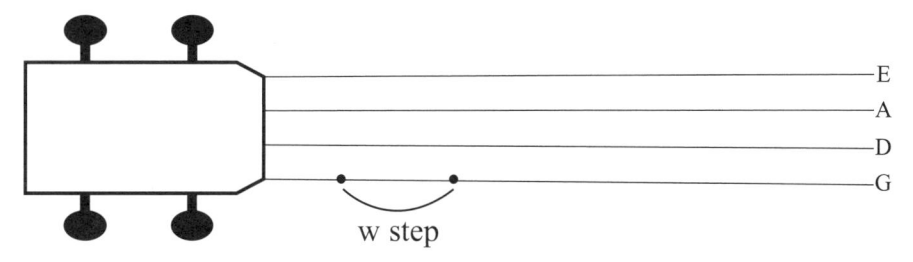

w step

E
A
D
G

A whole step is the same distance in sound on all instruments.

Sound Advice Level 1 — Lesson 19 Learning Guide

LESSON 19 Learning Guide

Major and Minor 2nds

When the upper note of a whole step (W) is lowered a half step, the interval becomes a half step ($\frac{1}{2}$).

When the upper note of a major 2nd (maj 2) is lowered a half step, the interval becomes a minor 2nd (min 2).

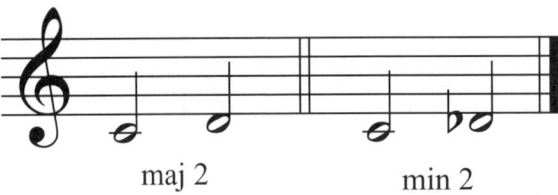

maj 2   min 2

Major 2nds are whole steps

B C D E F G A B C
  W   W   W

Minor 2nds are half steps

B C D E F G A B C
 $\frac{1}{2}$ $\frac{1}{2}$ $\frac{1}{2}$

The Sound of the Minor 2nd

From now on, the interval identification question in your ear-training worksheets will include minor 2nds. To learn the sound of this interval, sing the pairs of intervals below. Use the syllables do–re and do–ra.

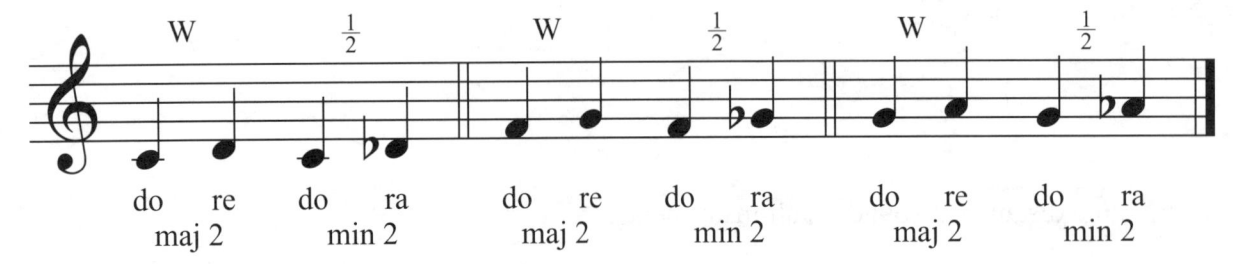

| W | $\frac{1}{2}$ | W | $\frac{1}{2}$ | W | $\frac{1}{2}$ |

do re   do ra   do re   do ra   do re   do ra
maj 2   min 2   maj 2   min 2   maj 2   min 2

Learning Guide

LESSON 19

You can also learn the sound of the minor 2nd by playing it on your instrument. Play a major 2nd (whole step), then lower the top note by a half step to create a minor 2nd. Compare the sound of the two intervals.

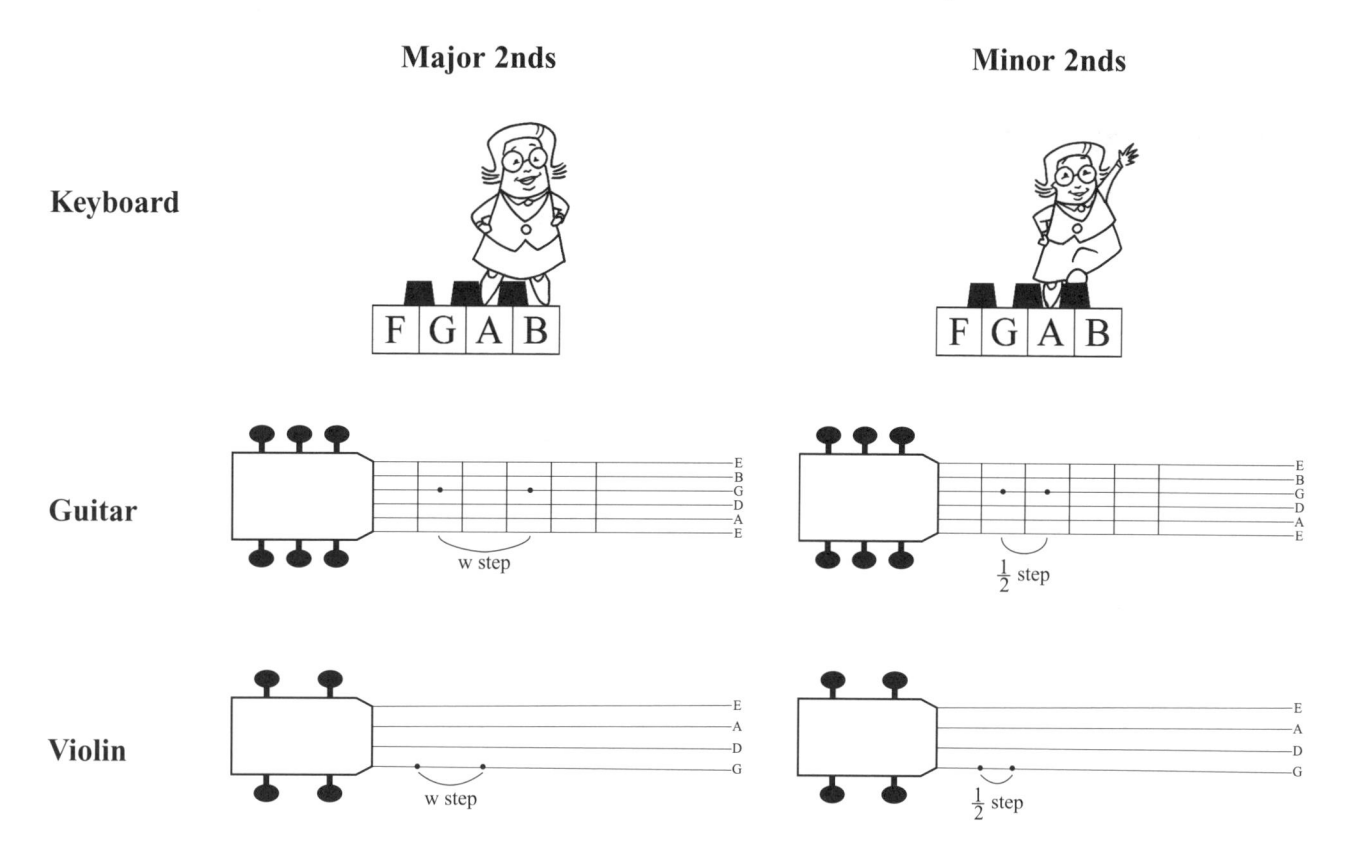

	Major 2nds	**Minor 2nds**
Keyboard	F G A B	F G A B
Guitar	w step	½ step
Violin	w step	½ step

Place a ✔ beside the minor 2nd on your Song Clue Chart on p.117.

Sound Advice Level 1   Lesson 19 Learning Guide   83

LESSON 19 Theory Worksheet

1 Draw a curved arrow from each marked key to the key a whole step (maj 2) higher. Name the second note. The first one has been done for you.

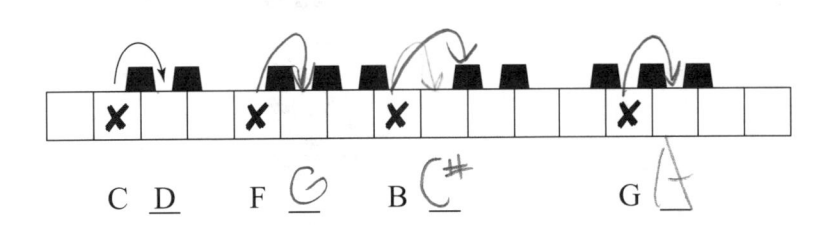

C D   F G   B C#   G A

2 Draw a curved arrow from each marked key to the key a half step (min 2) higher. Name second note. Compare this pattern to your answer for Question 1.

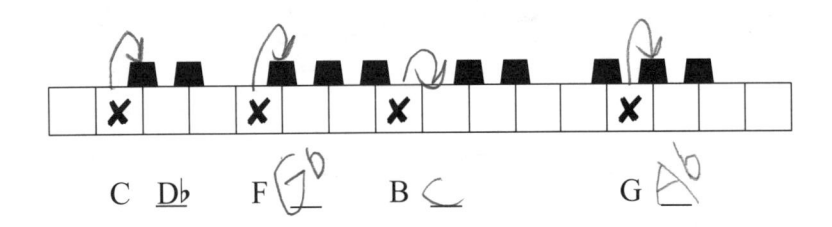

C Db   F Gb   B C   G Ab

3 Identify the following intervals as either whole steps (W) or half steps ($\frac{1}{2}$). Name the intervals as major 2nds or minor 2nds. The first one is done for you.

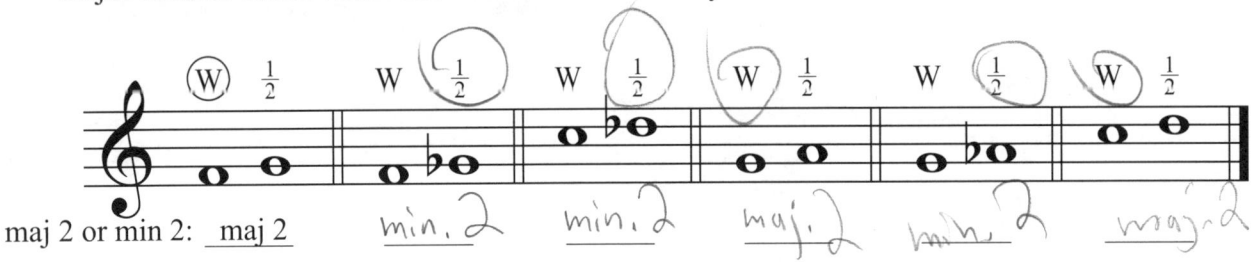

W ½   W ½   W ½   W ½   W ½   W ½

maj 2 or min 2: maj 2   min 2   min 2   maj 2   min 2   maj 2

4 Write the following intervals above the given notes.

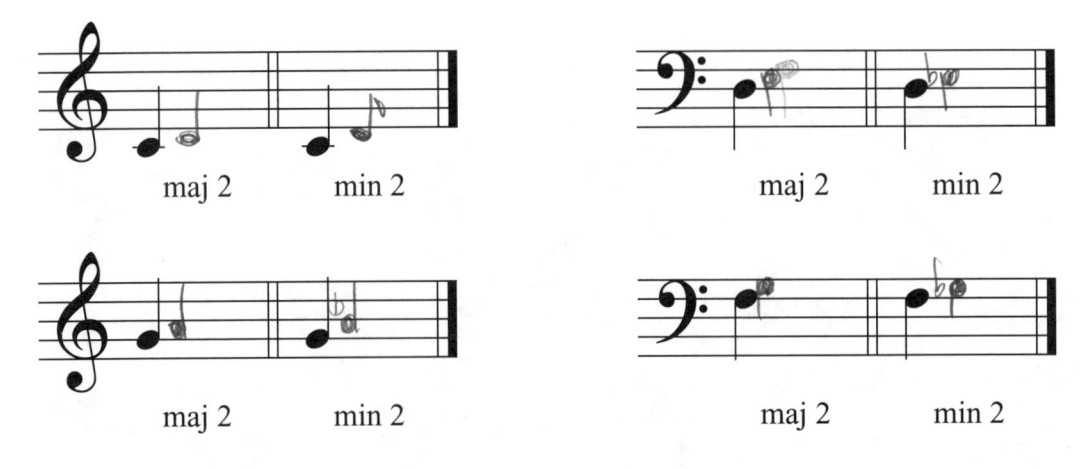

maj 2   min 2   maj 2   min 2

maj 2   min 2   maj 2   min 2

Theory Worksheet

LESSON 19

5 Complete the following chart by writing one note that equals the total value.

1 quarter note	+	2 eighth notes	=	
1 quarter note	+	1 quarter note	=	
1 half note	+	1 quarter note	=	
1 eighth note	+	1 eighth note	=	

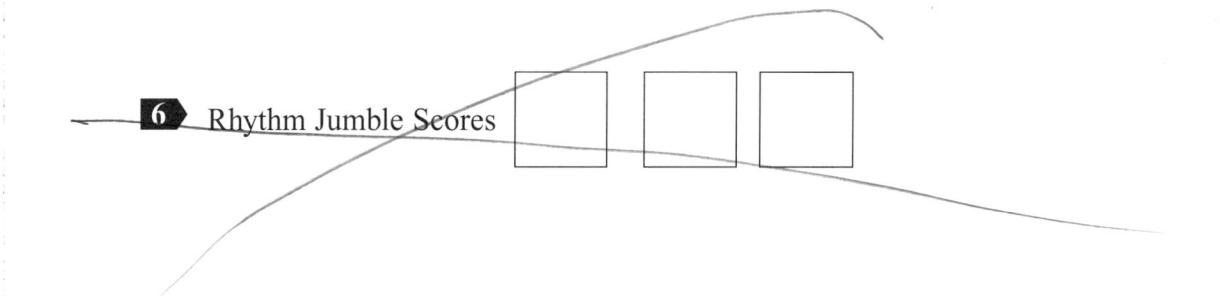

6 Rhythm Jumble Scores ☐ ☐ ☐

Sound Advice Level 1   Lesson 19 Theory Worksheet   85

LESSON 19

Ear-Training Worksheet

Track 94

1) Interval Identification: Identify the intervals you hear as maj 2nds or min 2nds.

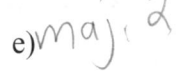

a) min 2   b) maj 2   c) maj 2   d) min 2   e) maj 2

Track 95

2) Rhythmic Reading:
a) Pause the recording. Sing the following rhythmic pattern while you tap a steady quarter-note beat.
b) Turn to the answer key and sing along with the recording.

Track 96

3) Rhythm Clapback: Clap the *rhythm* of the melody you hear from memory.

I LISTENED [1] TIMES

Track 97

4) Sight Singing:
a) Pause the recording. Sing the following scale while you tap a steady quarter-note beat.
b) Turn to the answer key and sing along with the recording.

Track 98

5) Melodic Dictation: Sing back the melody you hear from memory, then write it on the staff below. The melody is in 2/4 time and begins on Middle C.

I LISTENED [ ] TIMES

Track 99

6) Error Detection: Circle any notes in the following melody that are not played correctly.

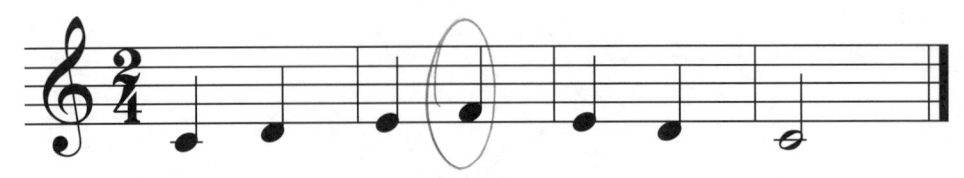

86   Lesson 19 Ear-Training Worksheet   Sound Advice Level 1

Learning Guide

LESSON 20

Whole Steps and Half Steps in the Major Scale

Major scales can start on any note. All major scales sound the same because they have the same pattern of whole steps and half steps:

W W ½ W W W ½

Memorize this pattern.

The C Major Scale

When you play a C major scale on a keyboard, you start on C. You need only white keys for the pattern of whole and half steps.

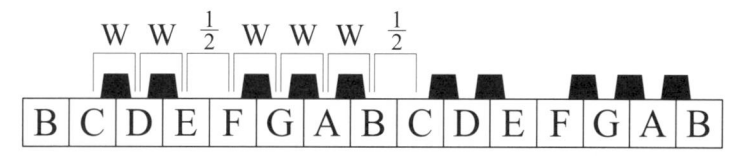

Scale Spelling: C D E F G A B C

The G Major Scale

When you play a G major scale on a keyboard, you start on G. You need an F♯ for the pattern of whole and half steps.

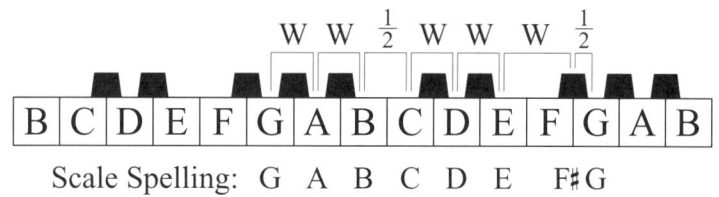

Scale Spelling: G A B C D E F♯ G

The F Major Scale

When you play an F major scale on a keyboard, you start on F. You need a B♭ for the pattern of whole and half steps.

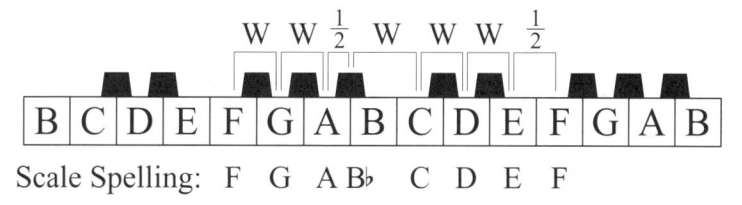

Scale Spelling: F G A B♭ C D E F

When you spell a scale, include all the letter names, and use each letter name only once. (The starting note is repeated at the top of the scale.)

Play the C, F, and G major scales on a keyboard. Even though they start on different notes, the scales "sound the same" because they all use the same pattern of whole and half steps.

Sound Advice Level 1   Lesson 20 Learning Guide

LESSON 20 — Theory Worksheet

1. Write the pattern of whole and half steps that make up a major scale.

W   W   ½   W   W   W   ½

2. a) Draw curved arrows on the keyboard below to create a G major scale. The first arrow has been drawn for you. Use the pattern in Question 1 as a guide.

b) Add any accidentals you need to create a G major scale. Use the keyboard above as a guide.

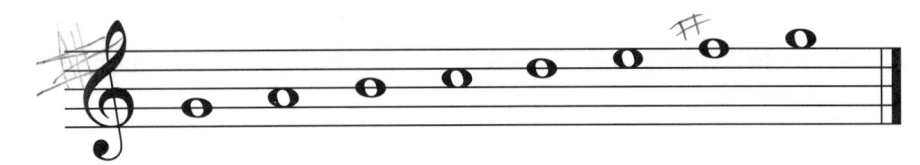

3. a) Draw curved arrows on the keyboard below to create an F major scale. The first arrow has been drawn for you. Use the pattern from Question 1 as a guide.

b) Add any accidentals you need to create an F major scale. Use the keyboard above as a guide.

4. Circle the quarter-note beats. Add bar lines according to the time signature and number the measures.

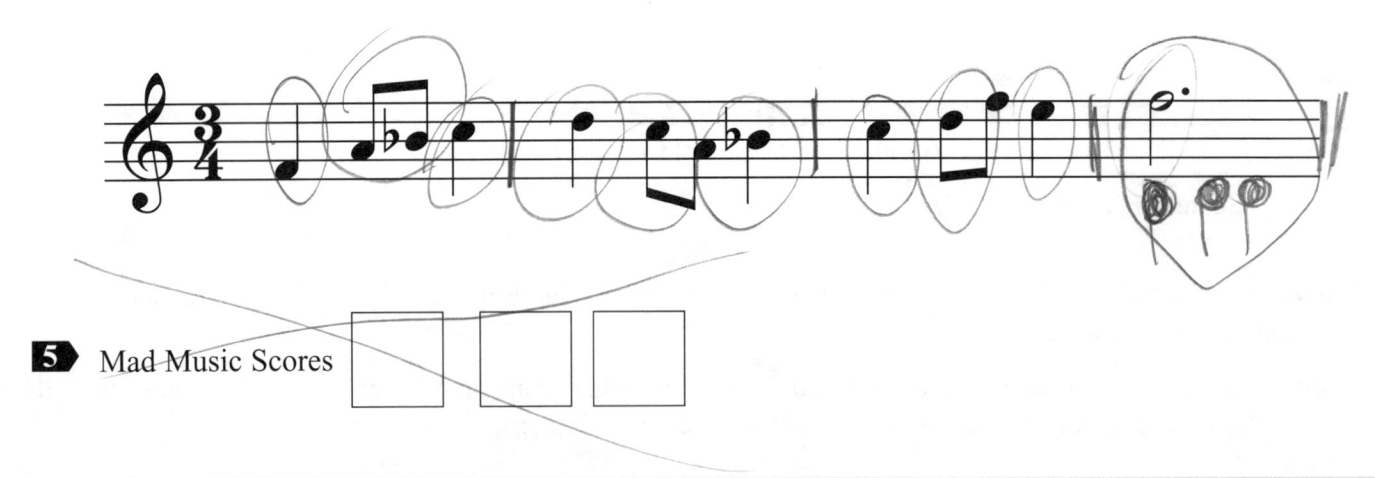

5. Mad Music Scores

88   Lesson 20 Theory Worksheet   Sound Advice Level 1

Ear-Training Worksheet

LESSON 20

Track 100

1. Sight Singing:
   a) Pause the recording. Sing the following scale while you tap a steady quarter-note beat.
   b) Turn to the answer key and sing along with the recording.

Track 101

2. Scale Identification: You will hear four scales. Identify each scale as major or not major.

Scale no. 1	Scale no. 2	Scale no. 3	Scale no. 4
☒ major	☐ major	☐ major	☐ major
☐ not major	☐ not major	☐ not major	☐ not major

Track 102

3. Rhythmic Dictation: Clap the *rhythm* of the melody you hear from memory, then write the rhythm in the space below. The rhythm is in 2/4 time.

I LISTENED 1 TIMES

Track 103

4. Melodic Dictation: Sing back the melody you hear from memory, then write it on the staff below. The melody is in 3/4 time and begins on Middle C.

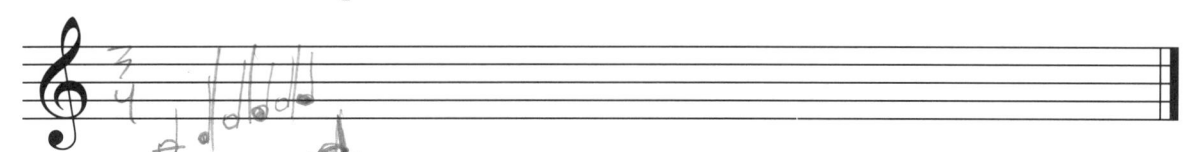

I LISTENED 2 TIMES

Track 104

5. Meter Identification: Identify the meter of the examples you hear as duple or triple. Tap a steady quarter-note beat as you listen.

   a) ☒ duple   b) ☐ duple
      ☐ triple   ☒ triple

Sound Advice Level 1 — Lesson 20 Ear-Training Worksheet

LESSON 21

Learning Guide

Facts about Accidentals

- An accidental is a symbol that alters the pitch of a note.
- Accidentals are always placed *in front of* the note.
- A sharp sign (♯) raises a note by one half step
- A flat sign (♭) lowers a note by one half step.
- An accidental placed in front of a note stays in effect until the next bar line. A bar line cancels all accidentals used in the previous measure.
- Accidentals alter *only* the pitch of the note that they are in front of. For example, a sharp in front of Middle C does not affect any other C on the staff.

Accidentals: The Natural Sign ♮

If you want to cancel an accidental before the next bar line, use a **natural sign**.

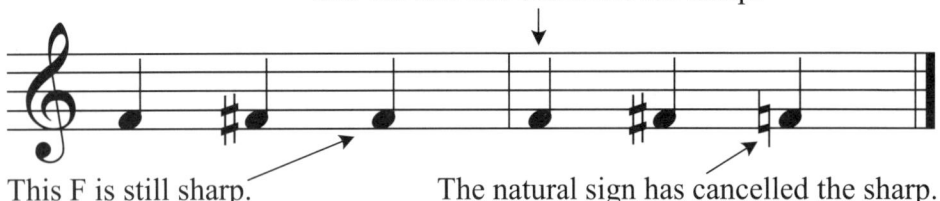

The bar line has cancelled the sharp.

This F is still sharp.   The natural sign has cancelled the sharp.

How to Draw a Natural Sign

1 Draw an "L" but tilt the bottom line up at a slight angle.

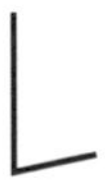

2 Halfway up the "L," draw a bent line that looks like the number "7."

3 Place the natural sign *in front of* the note it alters.

4 Place the natural sign on the *same line or space* as the notehead. If you cover the notehead, you should still be able to tell which note is to be altered.

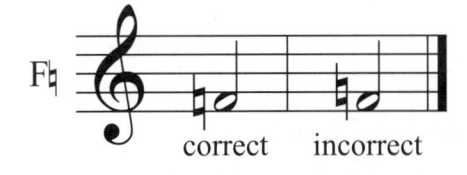

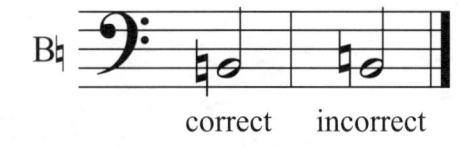

F♮   correct   incorrect   B♮   correct   incorrect

90   Lesson 21 Learning Guide   Sound Advice Level 1

Learning Guide

LESSON 21

Octaves (8ves)

You can find octaves on a keyboard, by counting eight white keys. Count the first key as "1." Because there are only seven different white-key names on the keyboard, the eighth white key always has the same letter name as the first.

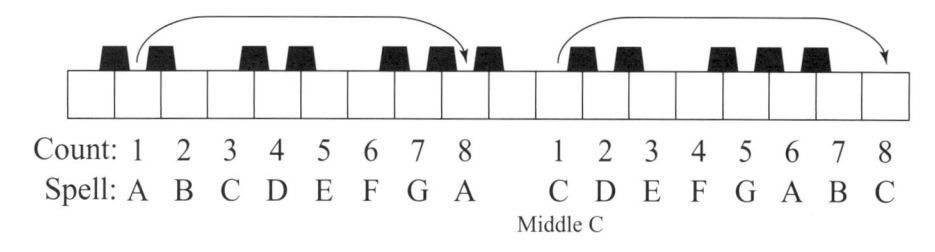

Count: 1 2 3 4 5 6 7 8   1 2 3 4 5 6 7 8
Spell: A B C D E F G A   C D E F G A B C
                         Middle C

To find an octave (8ve) on the staff, count up eight lines and spaces from the first note. Count the first note as "1." You can also spell eight letter names starting from the first note.

Because there are only seven different note names in the music alphabet, you always end up on the same letter you started. An octave up or down from C is C, and an octave up or down from D is D, and so on.

Count up: 1 2 3 4 5 6 7 8   Count up: 1 2 3 4 5 6 7 8
Spell: A B C D E F G A   Spell: C D E F G A B C

The Sound of the Perfect 8ve

From now on, the interval identification questions in your Ear-Training Worksheets will include perfect 8ves. To learn the sound of this interval, sing this scale. Use syllables or numbers.

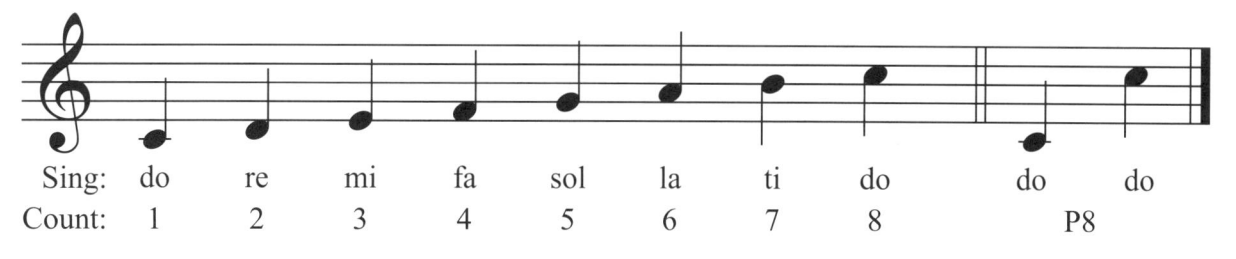

Sing: do re mi fa sol la ti do   do do
Count: 1 2 3 4 5 6 7 8   P8

Place a ✔ beside the perfect 8ve on your Song Clue Chart on p. 117.

Sound Advice Level 1   Lesson 21 Learning Guide

LESSON 21 Theory Worksheet

1 Trace the natural sign below, then draw five of your own. For extra practice, turn to the Drawing Symbols Chart on p.114 and draw some more.

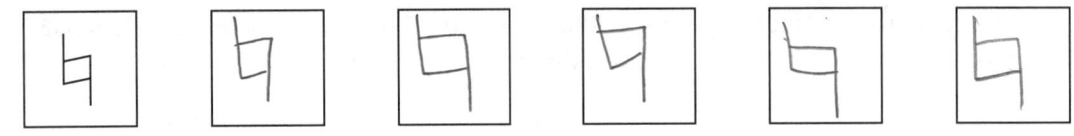

2 a) Write the following notes on the staff below. Remember to put the accidentals *in front of* the note, on the *same line or space* as the notehead.

b) Draw a line from each note on the staff below to its corresponding key on the keyboard.

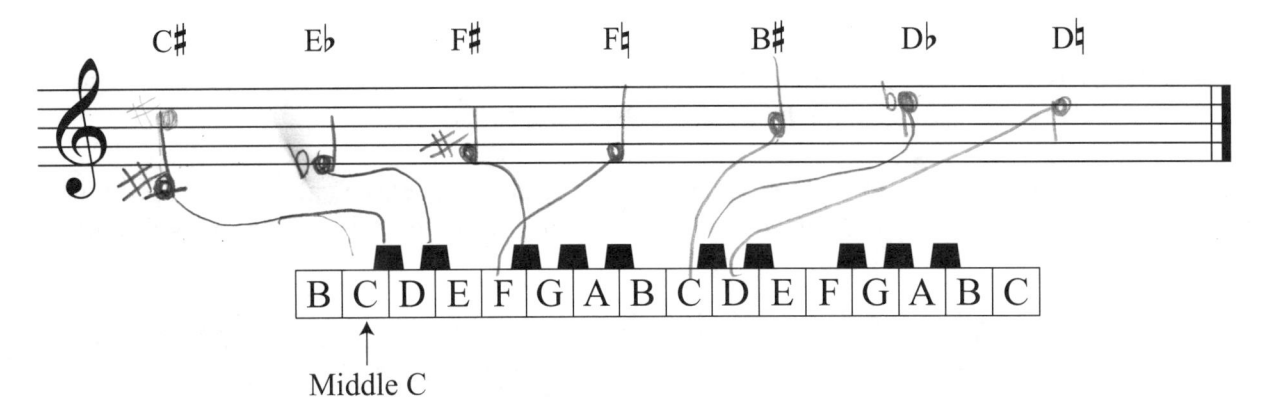

C#   Eb   F#   F♮   B#   Db   D♮

Middle C

3 Draw a line from each note on the staff above to its corresponding key on the keyboard. Middle C is marked.

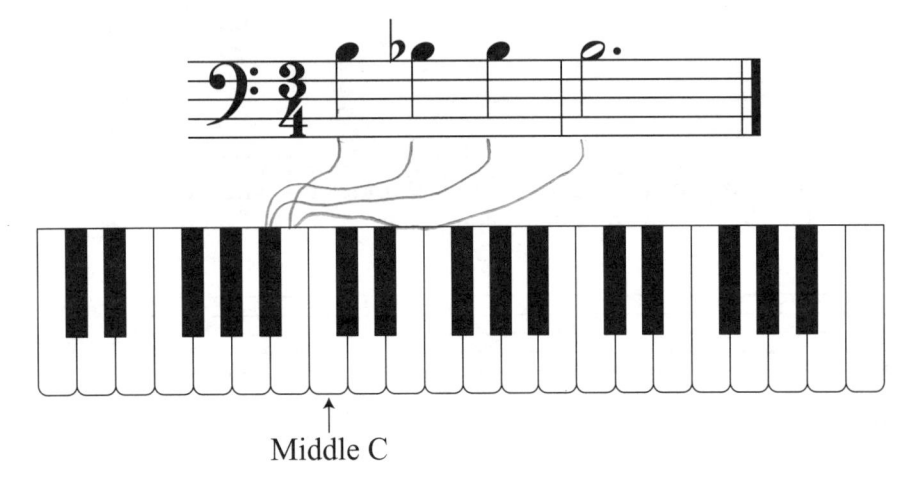

Middle C

4 Write perfect 8ves above each of the following notes.

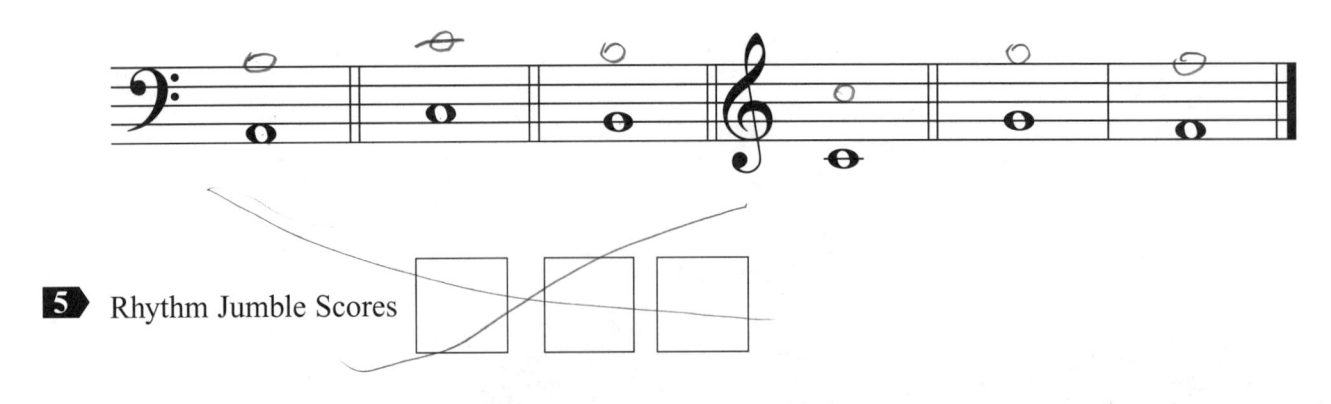

5 Rhythm Jumble Scores

92   Lesson 21 Theory Worksheet   Sound Advice Level 1

Ear-Training Worksheet — Lesson 21

1. Interval Identification: Identify the intervals you hear as min 2, maj 2, maj 3, P4, P5, or P8.

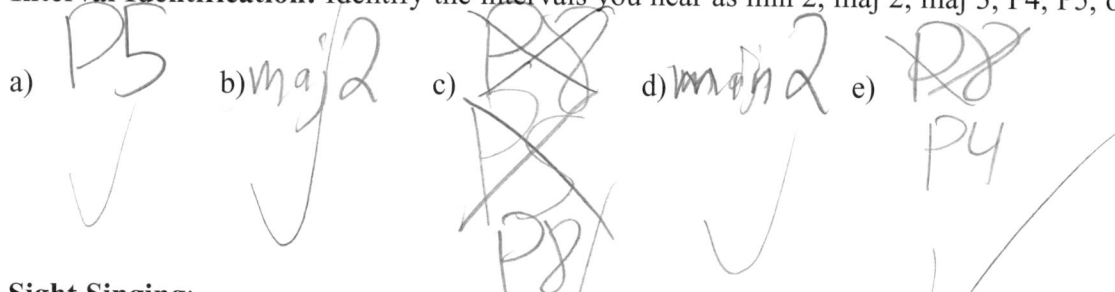

a) P5   b) maj 2   c) ~~P5~~ ~~P8~~   d) min 2   e) ~~P8~~ P4

2. Sight Singing:
a) Pause the recording. Sing the following melody while you tap a steady quarter-note beat.
b) Turn to the answer key and sing along with the recording.

3. Rhythm Clapback: Clap the *rhythm* of the melody you hear from memory. Record the number of times you listened.

4. Rhythmic Dictation: Clap the *rhythm* of the melody you hear from memory, then write the rhythm in the space below. The rhythm is in 3/4 time.

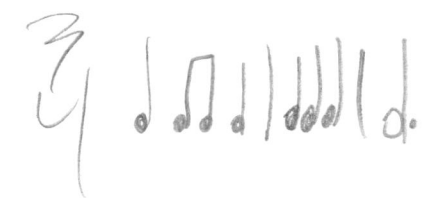

5. Melodic Dictation: Sing back the melody you hear from memory, then write it on the staff below. The melody is in 3/4 time and begins on Middle C.

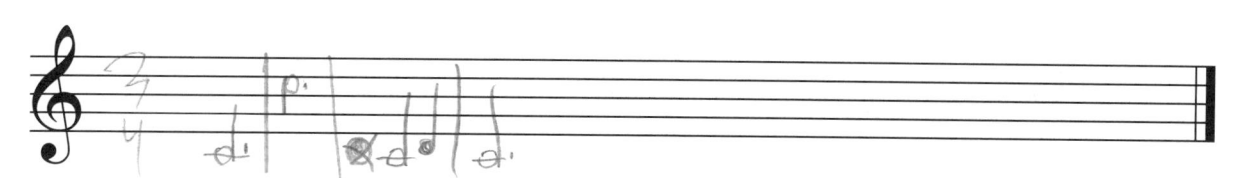

Lesson 22 Learning Guide

Quadruple Meter

When beats are grouped into a "strong–weak–medium–weak" pattern, we call it **quadruple meter**. In quadruple meter, there are **four beats** in each measure.

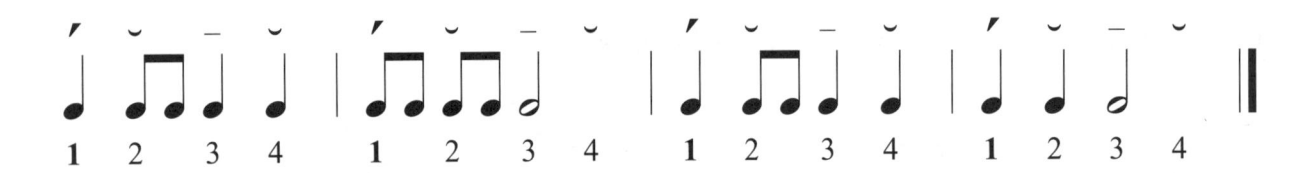

The accents are shown by the symbols ′ (strong), ˘ (weak), and − (medium).

New Time Signature 4/4

The top number of a time signature tells you the number of beats in each measure. The bottom number tells you what kind of note gets one beat.

$$\frac{4}{4} = \frac{4}{\text{♩}} \quad \begin{array}{l} \leftarrow \text{Number of beats} \\ \leftarrow \text{Beat note (♩)} \end{array}$$

4/4 is also called common time and can be written like this: **C**

The Whole Note o

This is a **whole note**: o

Whole notes have a notehead but no stem. Whole notes are held for four beats.

Sing these whole notes while you tap a steady beat:

o   o   o
ta - a - a - a   ta - a - a - a   ta - a - a - a

94   Lesson 22 Learning Guide   Sound Advice Level 1

Learning Guide

LESSON 22

The Whole Rest

A whole rest is equal in duration to a whole note or four quarter notes.

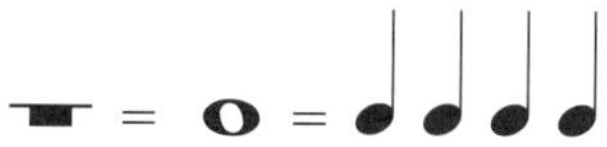

A whole rest is also used to show a whole measure of rest in any meter.

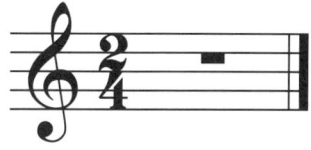

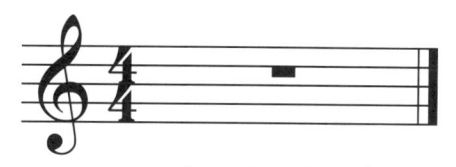

	sh - sh		sh - sh - sh		sh - sh - sh - sh
Count:	1 2	Count:	1 2 3	Count:	1 2 3 4

The Half Rest

A half rest is equal in duration to a half note or two quarter notes.

ta   ta   sh - sh

Hat

Half

Hole

Whole

Turn to the Rhythm Jumble Chart on p. 115 and circle the whole note, the whole rest, and the half rest. From now on, you can include them when you play Rhythm Jumble.

Sound Advice Level 1   Lesson 22 Learning Guide   95

LESSON 22 Theory Worksheet

1 Name the following intervals.

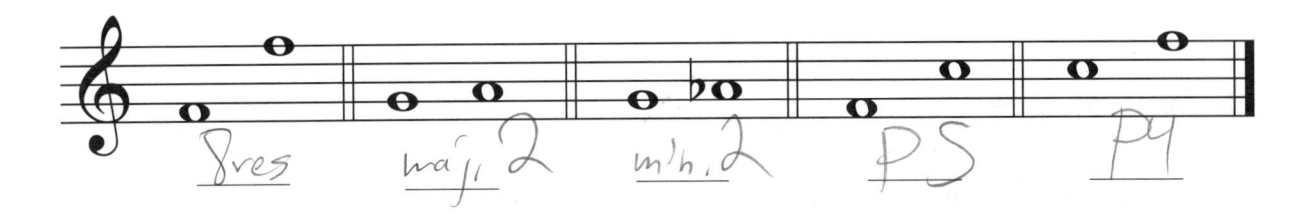

8ves, *maj. 2*, *min. 2*, *P5*, *P4*

2 Add bar lines to the following rhythmic patterns, then answer the questions.

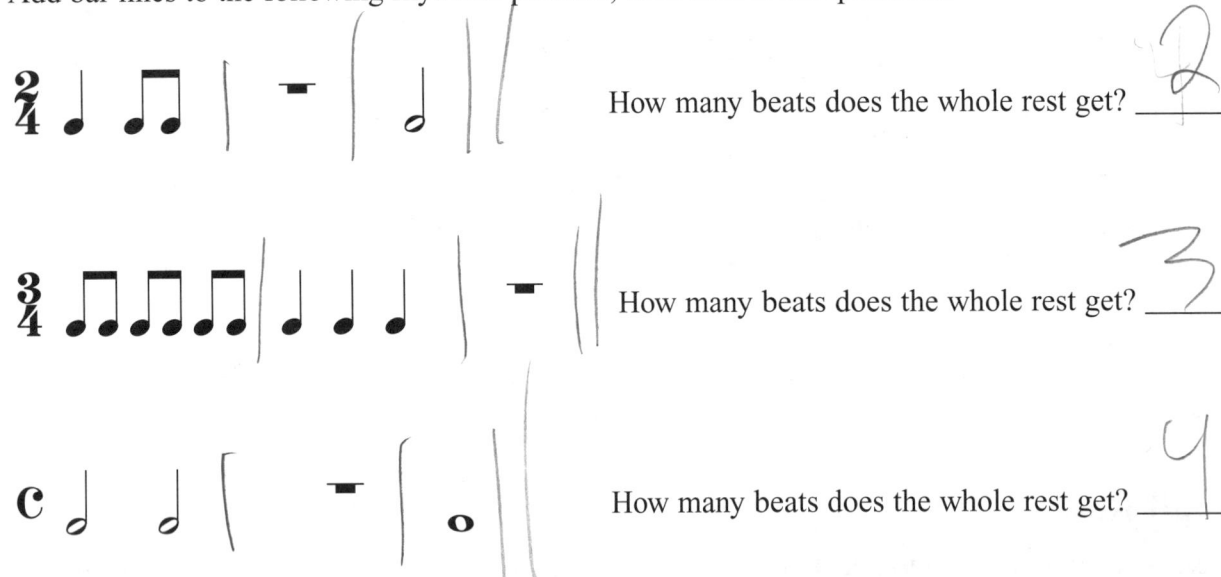

How many beats does the whole rest get? **2**

How many beats does the whole rest get? **3**

How many beats does the whole rest get? **4**

3 Draw a line from each symbol in the center to its name and number of beats.

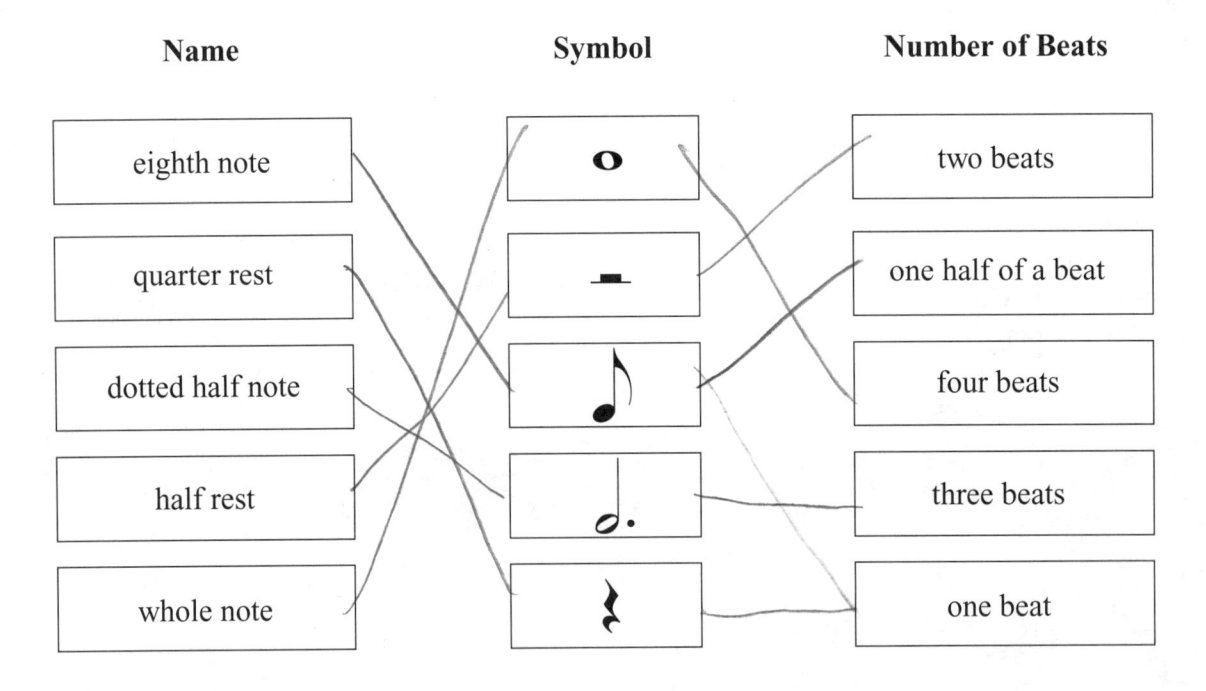

Name	Symbol	Number of Beats
eighth note	o	two beats
quarter rest	▬	one half of a beat
dotted half note	♪	four beats
half rest	𝅗𝅥.	three beats
whole note	𝄽	one beat

LESSON 22

Theory Worksheet

4 a) Draw curved arrows on the keyboard below to create a G major scale.

b) Add any accidentals you need to create a G major scale on the staff below. Use the keyboard above as a guide.

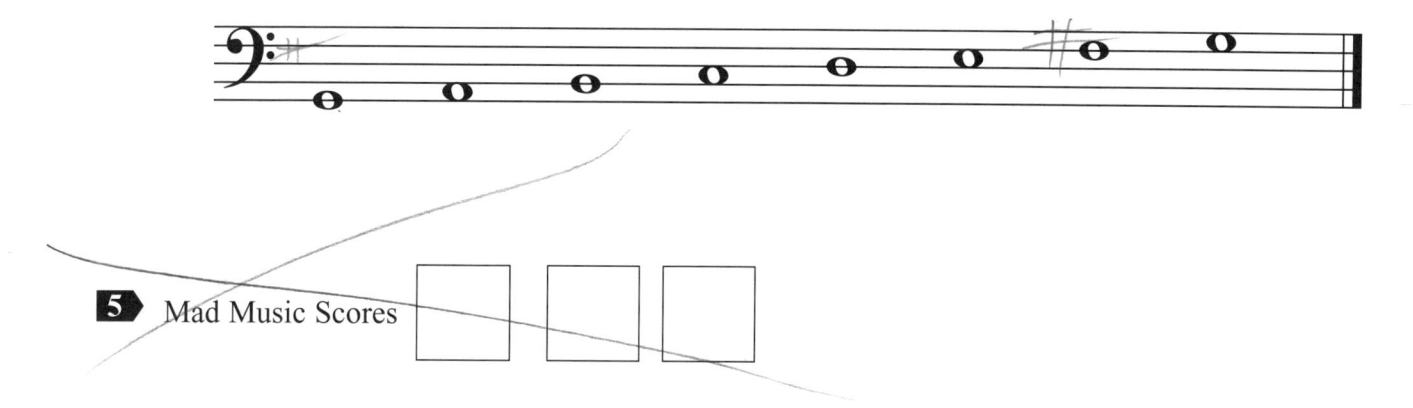

5 Mad Music Scores

Sound Advice Level 1

LESSON 22 — Ear-Training Worksheet

1) Interval Identification: Identify the intervals you hear as min 2, maj 2, maj 3, P4, P5, or P8.

a) maj. 2   b) P8   c) P4   d) P5   e) min. 2

2) Rhythmic Reading:
a) Pause the recording. Sing the following rhythmic pattern while you tap a steady quarter-note beat.
b) Turn to the answer key and sing along with the recording.

3) Rhythm Clapback: Clap the *rhythm* of the melody you hear from memory. Record the number of times you listened.

I LISTENED 1 TIMES

4) Sight Singing:
a) Pause the recording. Sing the following melody while you tap a steady quarter-note beat.
b) Turn to the answer key and sing along with the recording.

5) Melody Singback/Playback: Sing the melody you hear from memory, then play it back on your instrument. The melody begins on Middle C.

6) Error Detection: Circle any notes in the following melody that are not played correctly.

Learning Guide

LESSON 23

Key Signatures

Most composers base their compositions on scales. This means that the same accidentals are needed over and over again. One way to write music is to add an accidental every time you need to alter a note.

Another way is to put all the accidentals for the scale you are using at the beginning of each line of music. This pattern of accidentals is called a **key signature**. Key signatures go in front of time signatures.

Compare these two melodies. The first melody uses accidentals. The second melody has a key signature. Both melodies sound the same. Which one is easier to read?

On the grand staff, the key signature appears in both clefs. The sharps or flats are placed in specific locations. Here are some examples of key signatures.

C major   G major   F major

Play these three scales. They start on different notes, but they all sound the same. This is because all major scales have the same pattern of whole steps and half steps.

Key signature: C major (no accidentals)

Key signature: G major (one accidental—F sharp)

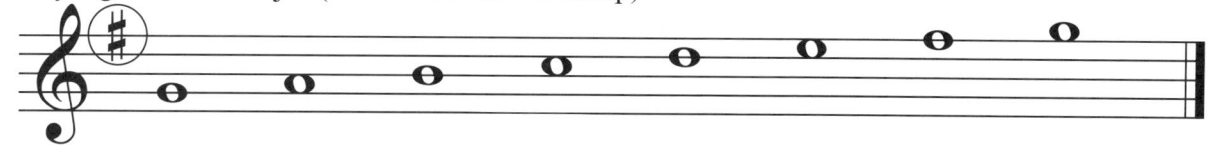

Key signature: F major (one accidental—B flat)

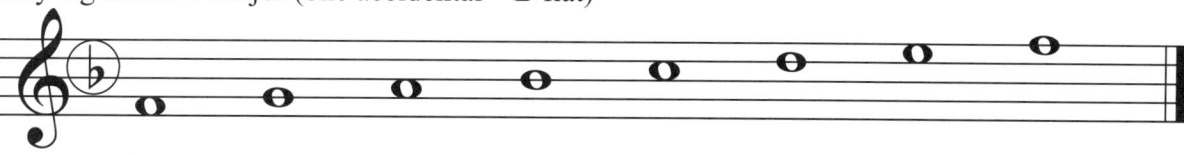

Sound Advice Level 1   Lesson 23 Learning Guide   99

LESSON 23 Theory Worksheet

1) Mark the whole steps (W) and half steps ($\frac{1}{2}$) in the following scales. The first one has been started for you.

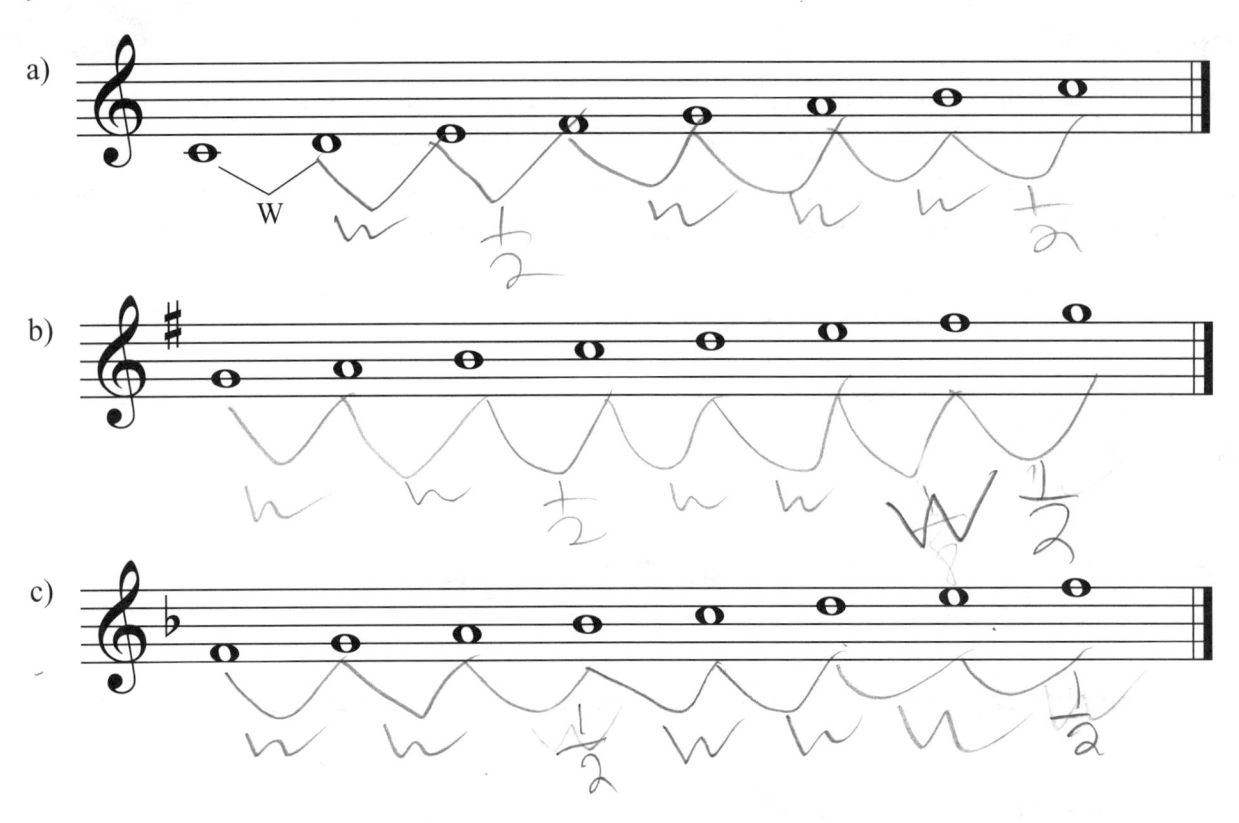

a) [C major scale on treble staff]
W W ½ W W W ½

b) [G major scale on treble staff]
W W ½ W W W ½

c) [F major scale on treble staff]
W W ½ W W W ½

2) Take a good look at the pattern of whole steps and half steps in the scales above. Write the pattern in the blanks below. You can use this pattern to create other major scales, starting on different notes.

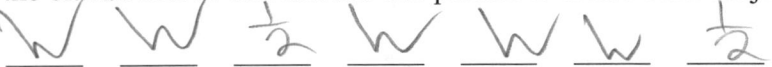

W   W   ½   W   W   W   ½

3) Draw key signatures for the following keys.

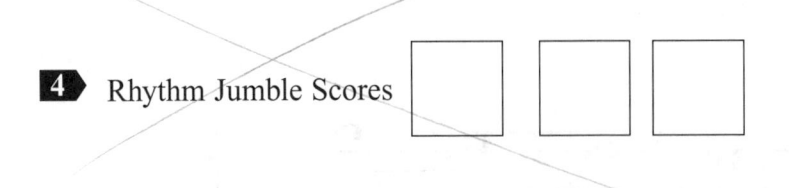

F major   C major   G major

4) Rhythm Jumble Scores [ ] [ ] [ ]

100 — Lesson 23 Theory Worksheet — Sound Advice Level 1

Ear-Training Worksheet
Lesson 23

1. Interval Identification: Identify the intervals you hear as min 2, maj 2, maj 3, P4, P5, or P8.

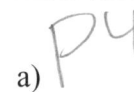

a) P4   b) min 2   c) P5   d) maj 3   e) P8

2. Sight Singing:
a) Pause the recording. Sing the following melody while you tap a steady quarter-note beat.
b) Turn to the answer key and sing along with the recording.

In G major, G is "do."

3. Melodic Dictation: Sing back the melody you hear from memory, then write it on the staff below. The melody is in G major, in 3/4 time, and begins on G.

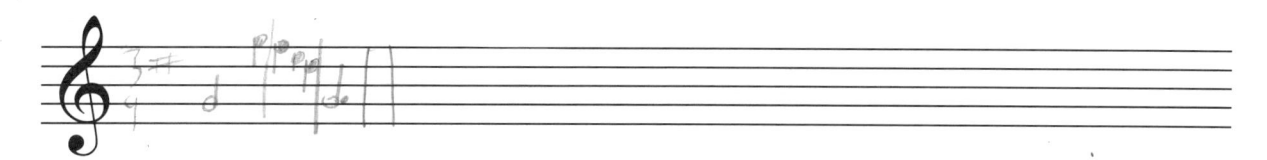

I LISTENED ___ TIMES

4. Scale Identification: You will hear four scales. Identify each scale as major or not major.

Scale no. 1	Scale no. 2	Scale no. 3	Scale no. 4
☒ major	☐ major	☒ major	☒ major
☐ not major	☒ not major	☐ not major	☐ not major

5. Meter Identification: Identify the meter of the following examples as duple or triple. Tap a steady quarter-note beat as you listen.

a) ☐ duple   b) ☒ duple
   ☒ triple   ☐ triple

Lesson 24 Learning Guide

Terms and Symbols

Composers often add terms or symbols to their music. These extra markings tell us how the music should sound: smooth or detached, loud or soft, fast or slow, and so on.

Here are some new terms and symbols for you to learn.

Legato

When notes are played smoothly and sound connected, we describe the sound as *legato*.

Slur

A **slur** is a curved line:

All the notes underneath or above a slur should be played *legato*. A slur can link two or three notes, or it can continue for several measures. Here are some examples.

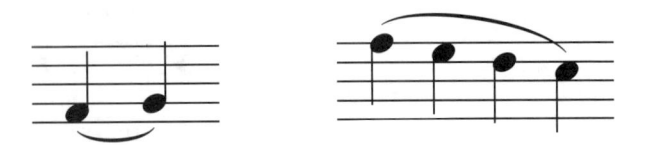

Be careful not to confuse a slur with a tie when there are only two notes.
- A tie connects two notes of the *same* pitch. The two notes are played as one longer sound.
- A slur connects notes of *different* pitches. The two notes are played *legato*.

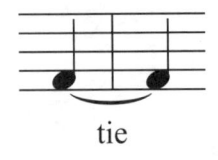

tie

slur

Staccato

When notes are played short and detached, we described the sound as **staccato**. *Staccato* is the opposite of *legato*.

The symbol for *staccato* is a dot placed directly above or below a notehead. *Staccato* dots always appear on the opposite side from the stem. If the stem goes up, the dot goes below. If the stem goes down, the dot goes above.

Correct: Incorrect:

Be careful not to confuse a *staccato* dot with a dot placed *beside* a notehead.

- A dot beside a notehead lengthens the value of the note by half its value. It does not affect the *way* the note is played.
- A dot above or below a notehead tells you that the note is to be played *staccato*. It does not affect the *value* of the note.

These notes are played *staccato*:

These notes are *not* played *staccato*:

LESSON 24 Theory Worksheet

1 Draw a line from each pair of tied notes to the single note of the same value.

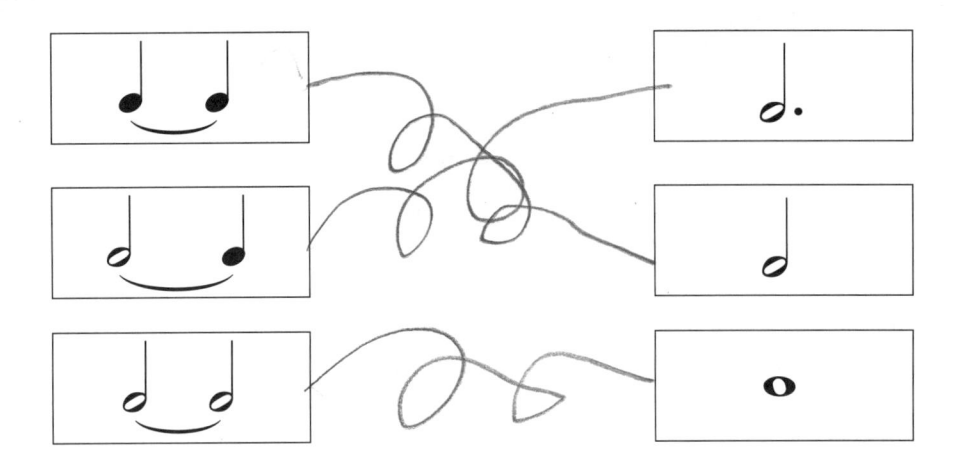

2 Identify the symbol below each pair of notes as either a tie or a slur.

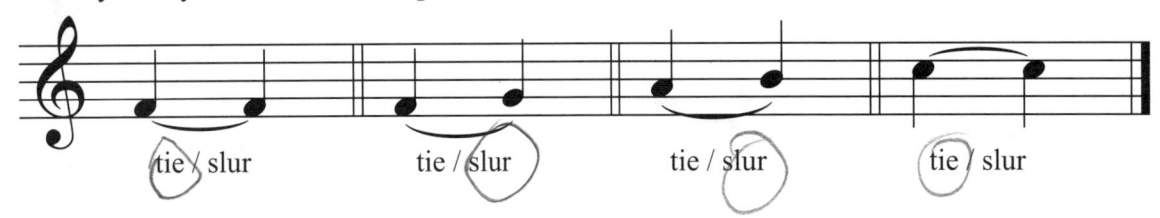

(tie) / slur   tie / (slur)   tie / (slur)   (tie) / slur

3 Identify the following intervals as either whole steps (W) or half steps ($\frac{1}{2}$). Name the intervals as major 2nds or minor 2nds.

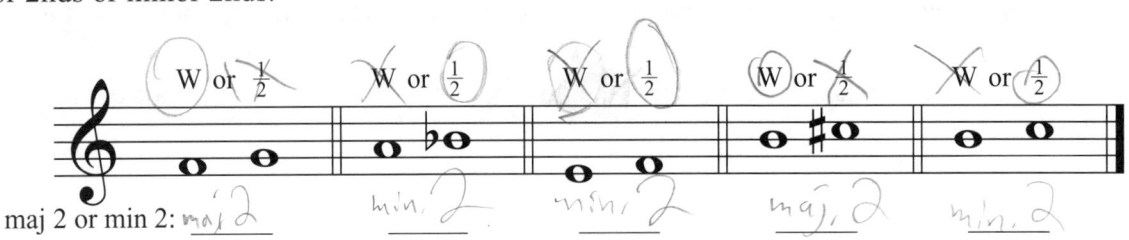

(W) or $\frac{1}{2}$ W or ($\frac{1}{2}$)   W or ($\frac{1}{2}$)   (W) or $\frac{1}{2}$ W or ($\frac{1}{2}$)

maj 2 or min 2: _maj 2_   _min 2_   _min 2_   _maj 2_   _min 2_

4
a) Number the measures in the following excerpt.
b) Name the note on the third beat of the third measure. __A__
c) Name the interval that is circled. __P4__
d) Name the major scale on which this melody is based. __C major__
e) Play this melody. Can you name the tune? __Don't Know__

5 Mad Music Scores

Lesson 24 Theory Worksheet   Sound Advice Level 1

Ear-Training Worksheet

Lesson 24

1. Interval Identification: The first note of each interval is given. Name the interval you hear, then write the second note.

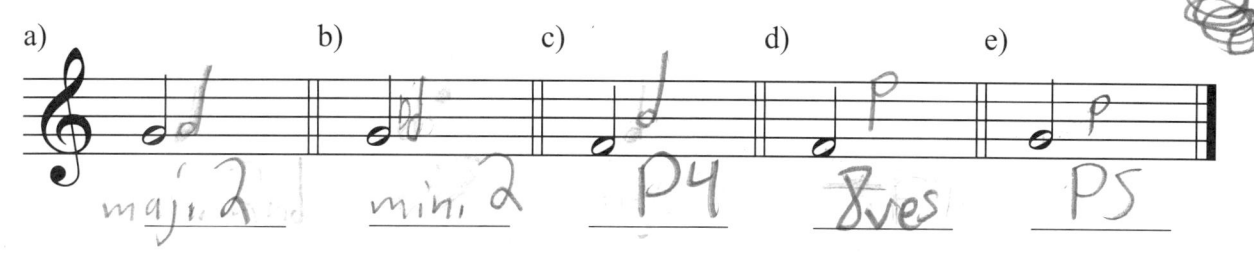

a) maj. 2   b) min. 2   c) P4   d) 8ves   e) P5

2. Sight Singing:
   a) Pause the recording. Sing the following melody while you tap a steady quarter-note beat.
   b) Turn to the answer key and sing along with the recording.

3. Melody Singback/Playback: Sing the melody you hear from memory, then play it back on your instrument. The melody is in F major, in 2/4 time, and begins on F.

4. Rhythmic Dictation: Clap the *rhythm* of the melody you hear from memory, then write the rhythm in the space below. The rhythm is in 4/4 time.

5. Error Detection: Circle any notes in this melody that are not played correctly. Rewrite the melody as it is played on the recording.

Theory Examination

Duration: one hour

Name: _Evan Balan_

5 1 Name the following notes.

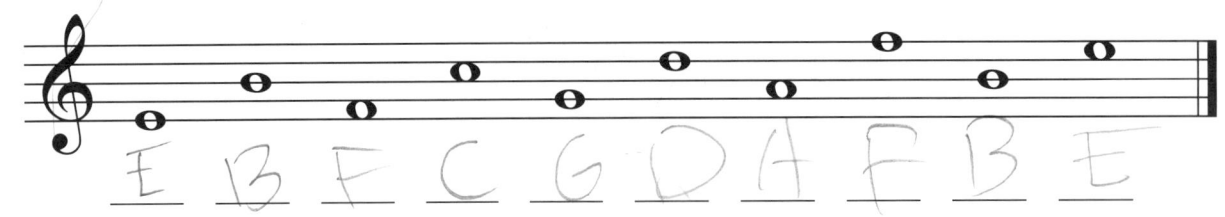

E B F C G D A F B E

5 2 Name the following notes.

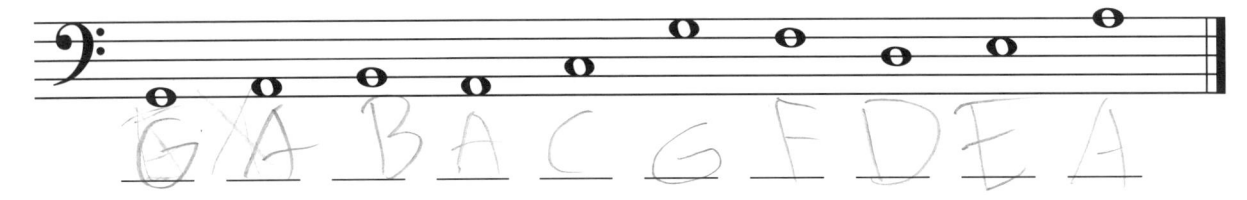

G A B A C G F D E A

5 3 Write the music alphabet, going up, in *steps* (2nds), starting on C.

C D E F G A

5 4 Write the music alphabet, going up, in *skips* (3rds) starting on D.

D F A C E G

5 5 Name the following intervals.

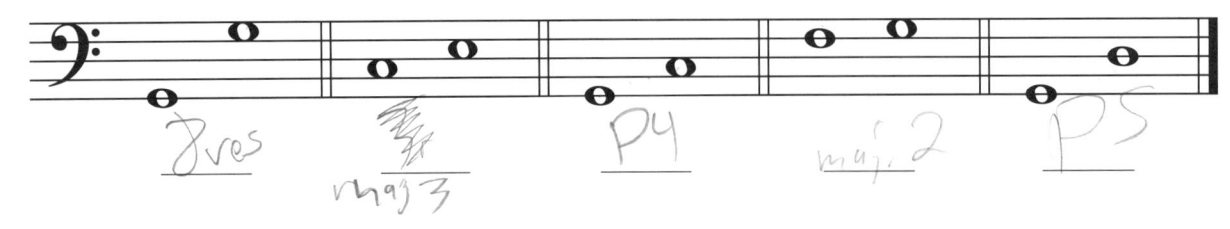

8ve / maj3 / P4 / maj2 / P5

5 6 Identify each pair of notes as a whole step (W) or a half step ($\frac{1}{2}$). Use the keyboard below to help you find the answers.

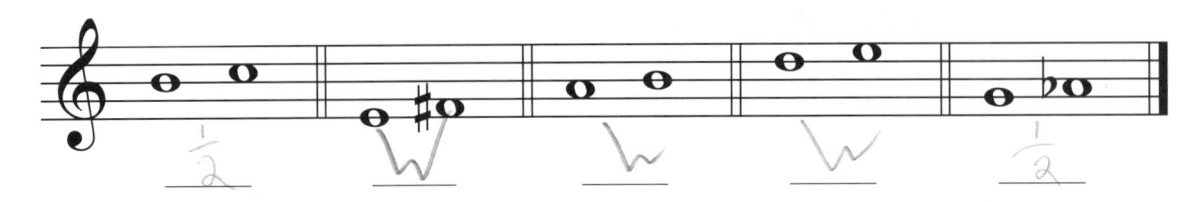

½ W W W ½

106 — Theory Examination — Sound Advice Level 1

Theory Examination

6 **7** Circle the quarter-note beats. Add bar lines according to the time signatures.

a) 2/4

b) C

c) 3/4

6 **8** Write the *ascending* major scales that belong to these key signatures. Use whole notes.

a)

b)

c)

4 **9** Fill in the blanks. The first one has been done as an example. Use the note-value chart below to help you find the answers.

There are	2	quarter notes in a half note.
There are	2	eighth notes in a half note.
There are	4	quarter notes in a whole note.
There are	8	eighth notes in a whole note.
There are	3	quarter notes in a dotted half note.

Note-Value Chart

Sound Advice Level 1   Theory Examination   107

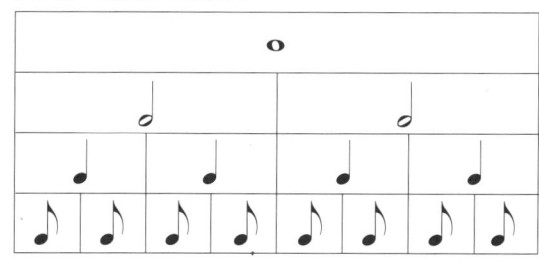

Theory Examination

4 **10** Draw a line from each sign to its name.

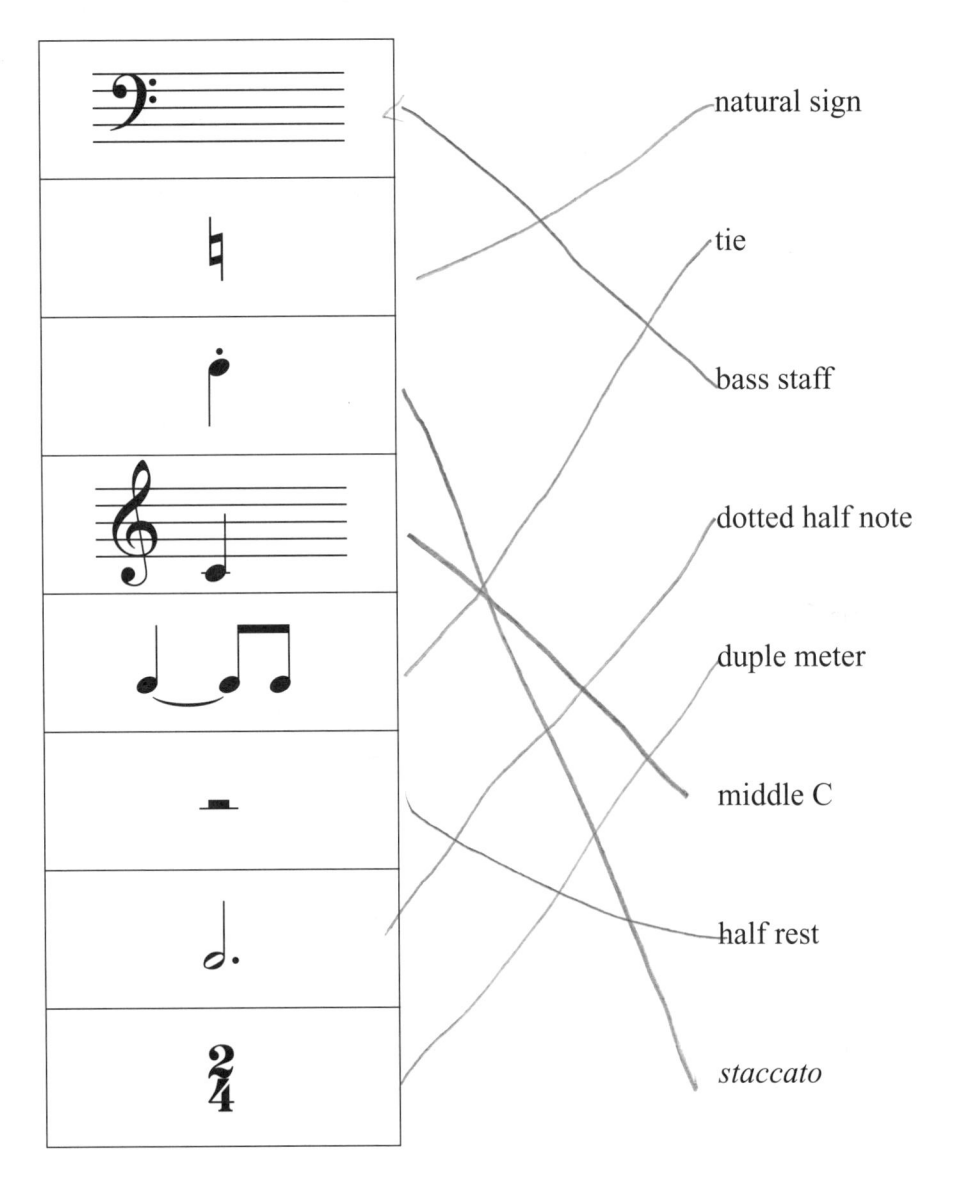

𝄢 (bass clef staff)	natural sign
♮	tie
(staccato note)	bass staff
(treble clef with middle C)	dotted half note
♩‿♫ (tied notes)	duple meter
▬ (half rest)	middle C
𝅗𝅥. (dotted half note)	half rest
2/4	*staccato*

50

108   Theory Examination   Sound Advice Level 1

Melody Master

These are the final Ear-Training Worksheets for Level 1. Spend as much time as you need to perfect these assignments. When you finish Melody Master, you are ready to move on to *Sound Advice* Level 2.

Melody Master consists of five sets of melodies. You need to complete all five sets using the three different methods described below. Finish all five sets with Method 1 before you go on to Method 2. Finish the five sets with Method 2 before you move on to Method 3. When you successfully complete each set, check the box at the bottom of this page to track your progress.

Always record your progress before going on to the next method!

Method 1: Melody Playback—Play What You Hear

Singers and instrumentalists can perform in their range. Each melody will be played twice on the recording. The key note (do) and the beat are given before each performance. The melodies start on the first, the second, or the third note of the scale.

Method 2: Sight Singing—Hear What You See

Turn to the Melody Master Answer Key and sight sing all five sets.

Method 3: Melodic Dictation—Write What You Hear

Write each melody on the staff. Each melody will be played twice. The key note (do) and the beat are given before each performance. The melodies start on the first, the second, or the third note of the scale.

Method 1: Playbacks	Method 2: Sight Singing	Method 3: Melodic Dictation
Set One ❏	Set One ❏	Set One ❏
Set Two ❏	Set Two ❏	Set Two ❏
Set Three ❏	Set Three ❏	Set Three ❏
Set Four ❏	Set Four ❏	Set Four ❏
Set Five ❏	Set Five ❏	Set Five ❏

Melody Master

Set One

Track 126

a) The following melody is in C major, 3/4 time.

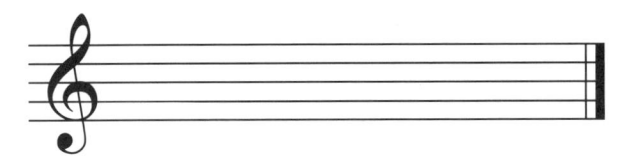

Track 127

b) The following melody is in F major, 3/4 time.

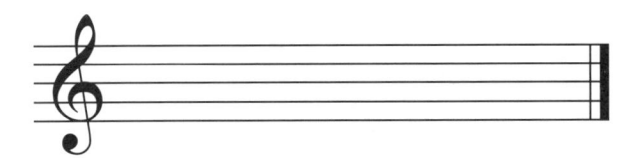

Track 128

c) The following melody is in G major, 3/4 time.

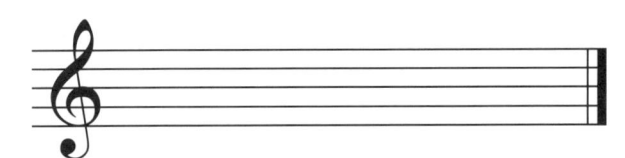

Track 129

d) The following melody is in F major, 3/4 time.

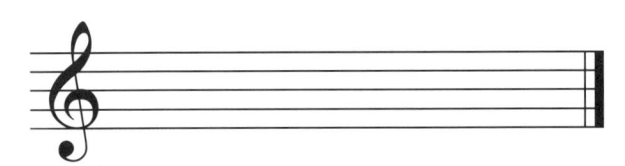

Track 130

e) The following melody is in C major, 3/4 time.

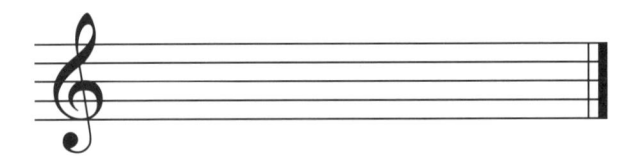

Check the appropriate box on p. 109.

Set Two

Track 131

a) The following melody is in C major, 3/4 time.

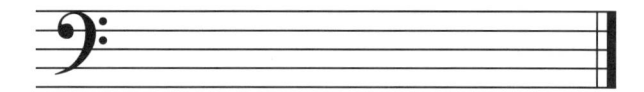

Track 132

b) The following melody is in G major, 3/4 time.

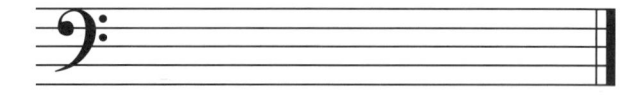

Track 133

c) The following melody is in F major, 3/4 time.

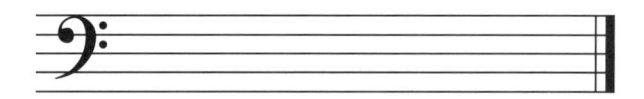

Track 134

d) The following melody is in G major, 3/4 time.

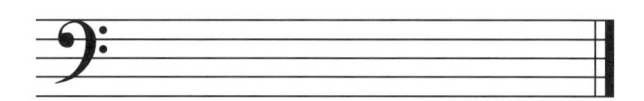

Track 135

e) The following melody is in C major, 3/4 time.

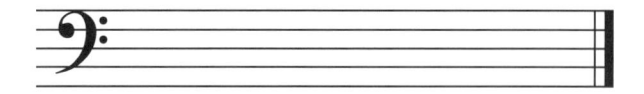

Check the appropriate box on p. 109.

Melody Master

Set Three

Track 136

a) The following melody is in G major, $\frac{2}{4}$ time.

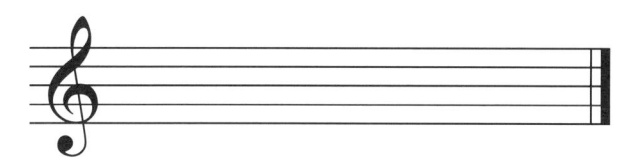

Track 137

b) The following melody is in F major, $\frac{2}{4}$ time.

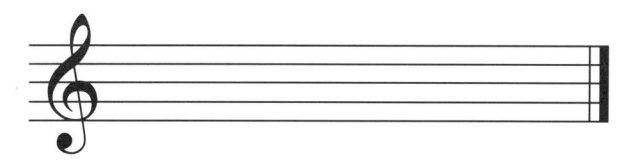

Track 138

c) The following melody is in C major, $\frac{3}{4}$ time.

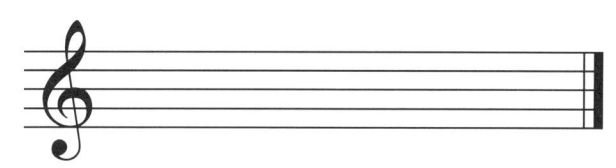

Track 139

d) The following melody is in G major, $\frac{2}{4}$ time.

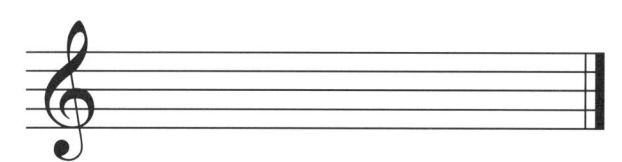

Track 140

e) The following melody is in F major, $\frac{2}{4}$ time.

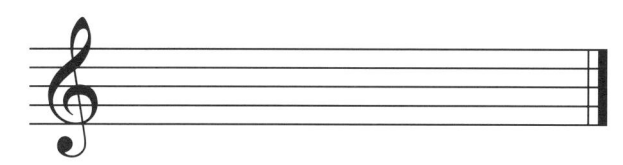

Check the appropriate box on p. 109.

Set Four

Track 141

a) The following melody is in F major, $\frac{2}{4}$ time.

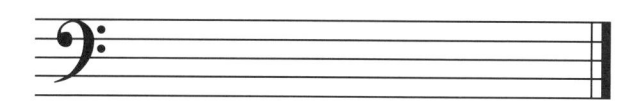

Track 142

b) The following melody is in G major, $\frac{3}{4}$ time.

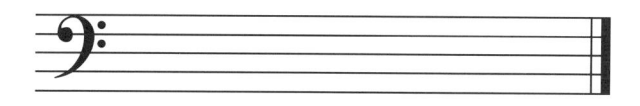

Track 143

c) The following melody is in C major, $\frac{3}{4}$ time.

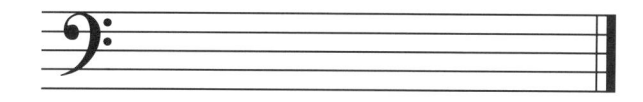

Track 144

d) The following melody is in F major, $\frac{2}{4}$ time.

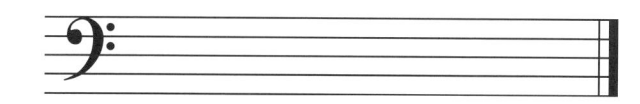

Track 145

e) The following melody is in G major, $\frac{3}{4}$ time.

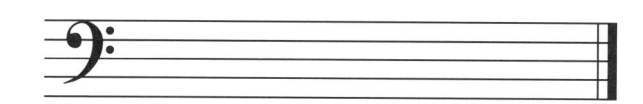

Check the appropriate box on p. 109.

Sound Advice Level 1 — Melody Master

Melody Master

Set Five

a) The following melody is in F major, 4/4 time.

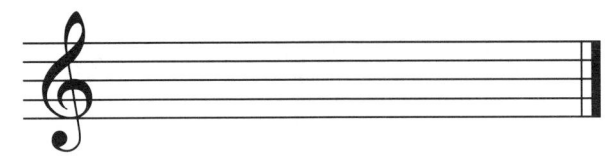

b) The following melody is in G major, 4/4 time.

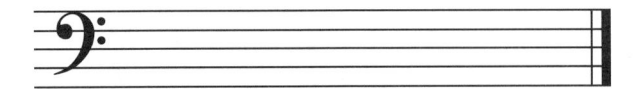

c) The following melody is in C major, 4/4 time.

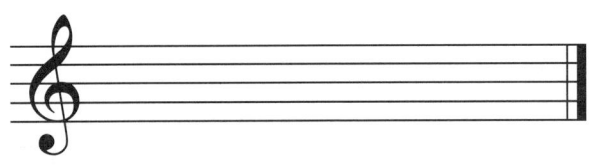

d) The following melody is in G major, 3/4 time.

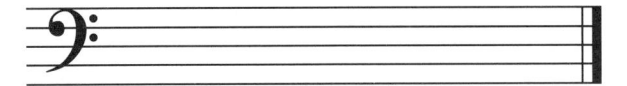

e) The following melody is in F major, 4/4 time.

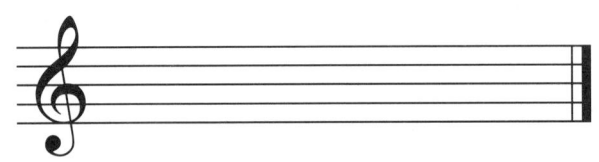

Check the appropriate box on p. 109.

Charts and Games

Note-Value Comparison Chart

This chart provides a visual illustration of how the various note values compare to each other. Refer to this chart each time you learn a new note or rhythmic unit.

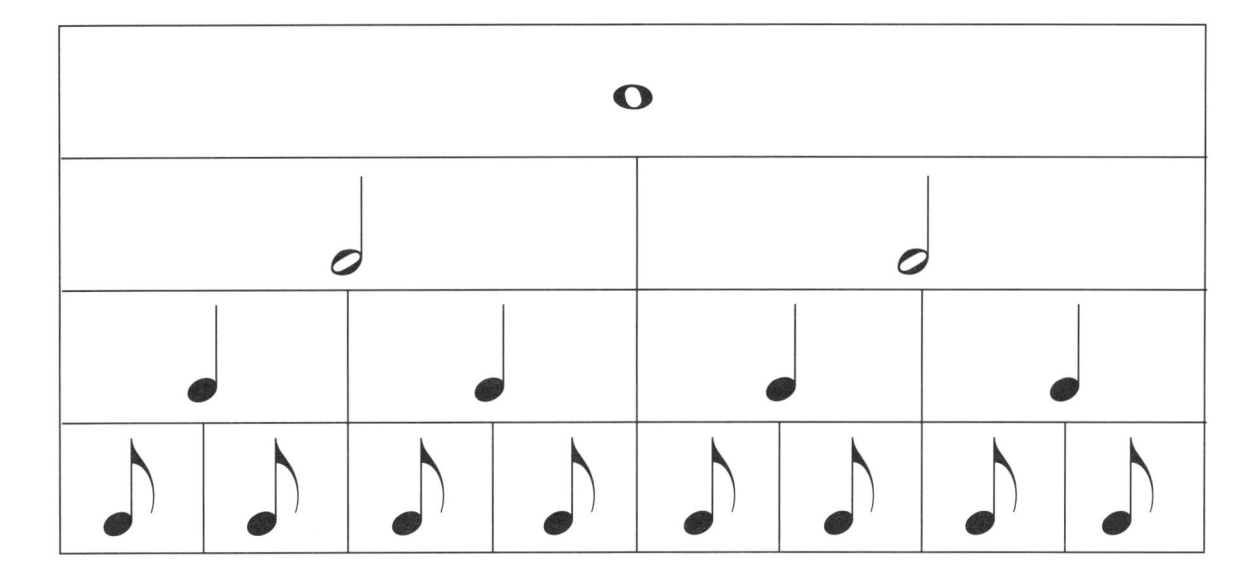

Charts and Games

Drawing Symbols Chart

This chart provides additional space for you to practice drawing various musical symbols. When a new symbol is introduced in a lesson, you will be instructed to turn to this chart to practice drawing them.

Practice tracing and then drawing the following clefs, accidentals, and rests.

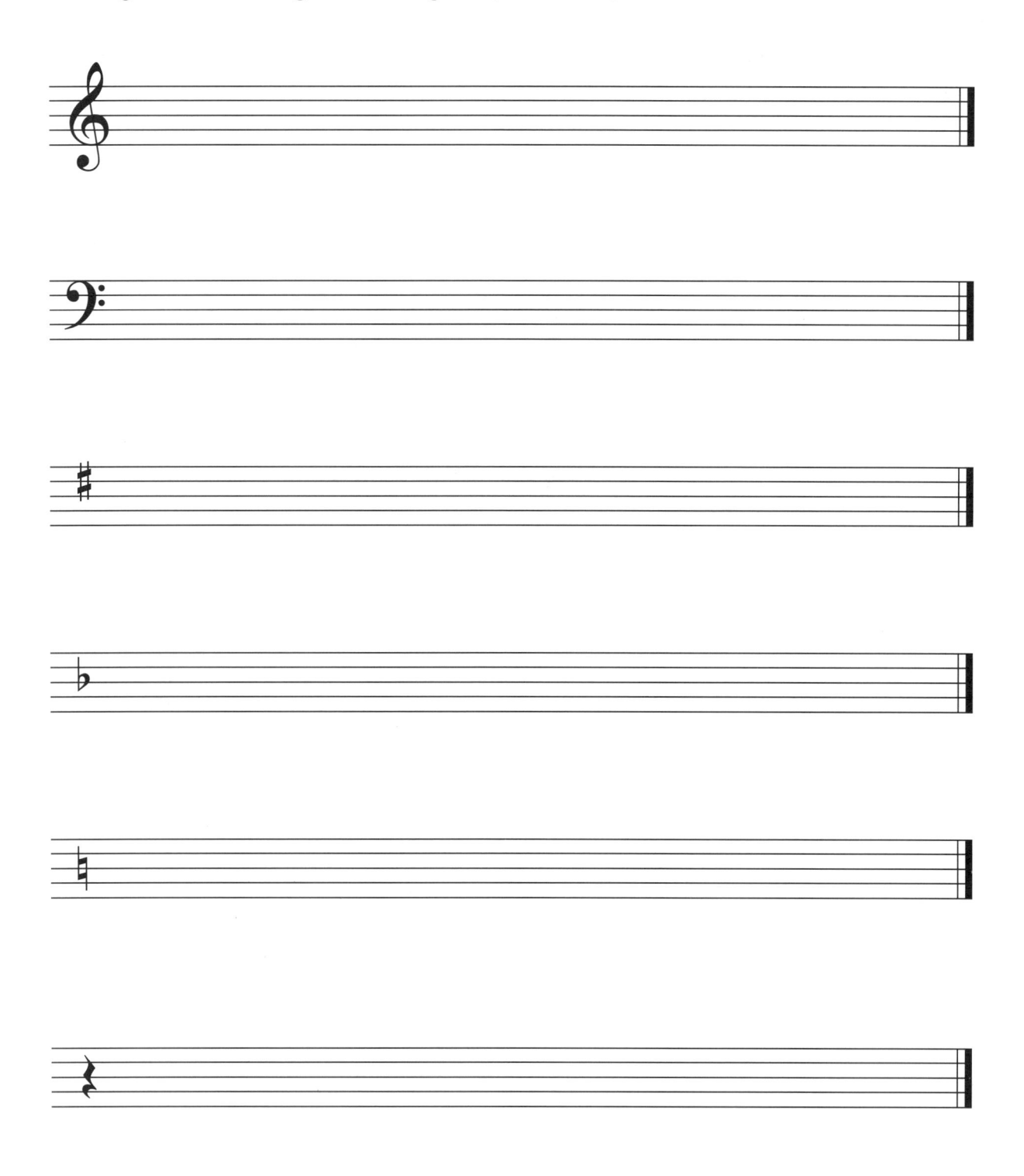

114 Charts and Games Sound Advice Level 1

Charts and Games

Rhythm Jumble Chart

Each time you learn a new rhythmic unit, circle it on the Rhythm Jumble Chart.

Use the Rhythm Jumble Chart to practice singing the circled rhythmic units every day. Tap the beat with your finger as you point to the rhythmic unit you are singing. Sing each unit two or three times before moving on to the next one. Gradually start mixing up the units by randomly pointing to different units. Try not to miss a beat!

You can also use this chart to play any of the Rhythm Jumble Games described on the next page.

Sound Advice Level 1 — Charts and Games — 115

Charts and Games

Rhythm Jumble Games

Rhythm Jumble Reading

The goal of this sight-reading game is to sing all the circled rhythmic units on the Rhythm Jumble chart in random order, while keeping a steady beat. To play Rhythm Jumble, you will need someone to keep track of the number of units you can sing correctly without stopping. You win the game when you can sing at least one more unit than the last time you played. Record your score in the Rhythm Jumble score box on your Theory Worksheet. When you can sing 25 units correctly, you will earn the official title of Rhythm Jumble "Reading Expert" and you may write the letters "RE" in the score box.

The rules are:
1) Tap a steady beat with your finger.
2) Point to each rhythmic unit as you sing it.
3) Sing a unit only twice before you move to a new one.
4) Sing the units in random order.
5) You are "out" if you sing a unit incorrectly or if your steady beat falters.

As you become more proficient, you can make the Rhythm Jumble game more challenging by increasing the tempo. You can also change rule 3 so that you sing a unit only once before you move on to the next one. (Students in group classes can play this game in teams and adapt the rules to meet their needs.)

Rhythm Jumble Solitaire

The rules for Rhythm Jumble Solitaire are the same as for Rhythm Jumble Reading, but you can play this game without a helper. All you need is a timer. Keep track of the number of seconds that you can continuously sing rhythmic units in random order before you make a mistake or your steady beat falters. You win the game when you have increased your time from your previous score. Record your score in the Rhythm Jumble score box on your Theory Worksheet. When you can sing random units continuously for 30 seconds, you will earn the official title of Rhythm Jumble "Solitaire Expert" and you may write the letters "SE" in the score box on your Theory Worksheet.

Rhythm Jumble Composer

To play Rhythm Jumble Composer, you need to make a set of rhythm cards. Use the rhythmic units on the Rhythm Jumble Chart (p. 115). Draw each rhythmic unit on a blank card. Make one copy of the whole rest and three copies of all other units. You should have a total of 25 cards.

Compose your own rhythmic pattern by laying out a series of cards from left to right in any order you choose. You can also shuffle the cards to mix them up before laying them out. Tap a steady beat while you point to each card in turn and sing your new rhythmic pattern. Keep track of how many cards you can sing correctly without faltering in your steady beat. Record your score in the box on the Theory Worksheet. When you can correctly sing a pattern that uses all 25 cards, you will earn the official title of Rhythm Jumble "Composing Expert" and you may write the letters "CE" in the score box on your Theory Worksheet.

Charts and Games

Song Clue Chart

This chart shows ascending intervals and provides several song clue examples for each one. There is also space for you to add your own song clues. Each time you learn a new interval, turn to this chart and place a check beside the interval.

Ascending ↗

Interval	✔	Possible Song Clues	Your Own Clue
min 2		The Entertainer Fascination	
maj 2		*Are You* Sleeping? *Lon-don* Bridge	
maj 3		*Oh When* the Saints *Kum-ba*-ya	
P4		*Here Comes* the Bride *We Wish* You a Merry Christmas	
P5		Do *You Hear* What I Hear? Twin-*kle Twin*-kle Little Star	
P8		*Some-where* Over the Rainbow Oh *the Wea*-ther Outside is Frightful	

You can keep your chart up-to-date by adding current or popular song and movie themes such as *The Pink Panther* (min 2) or *Harry Potter* (maj 3).

Sound Advice Level 1 · Charts and Games · 117

Charts and Games

Mad Music Game

This timed note-reading game uses the note-naming sheets on pp. 119–121. The goal is to name all the notes on a sheet in two minutes or less. There are three levels of difficulty: A, B, and C. When you can name all the notes on the Level A sheet within two minutes, go to Level B. When you have mastered Level B, move to Level C. When you can name all the notes on the Level C sheet in two minutes or less, you will have earned the status of "Note-Naming Expert" for Level 1 and will be awarded the Certificate of Achievement. Go to www.soundadvicedirect.com to download the Certificate!

Beginning with Lesson 7, you will often be asked to record three Mad Music scores on your Theory Worksheet. This means that part of your homework assignment for that lesson is to play Mad Music at least three times. (When you have mastered Level C, you do not have to record any more Mad Music scores.)

The easiest way to play this game is to have someone follow the Answer Keys on pp. 149–151 while you name the notes out loud.

Charts and Games

Mad Music Level A

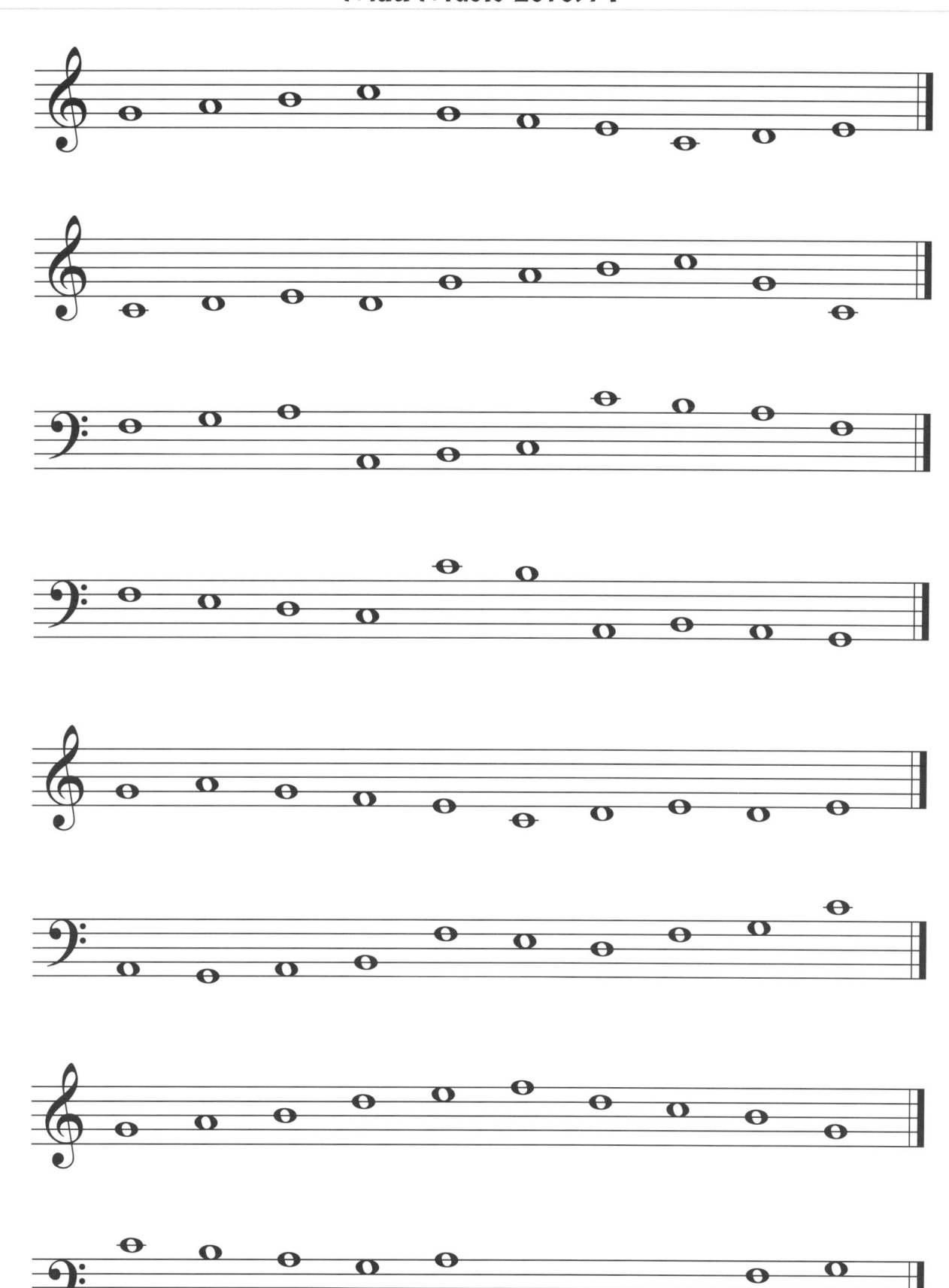

Charts and Games

Mad Music Level B

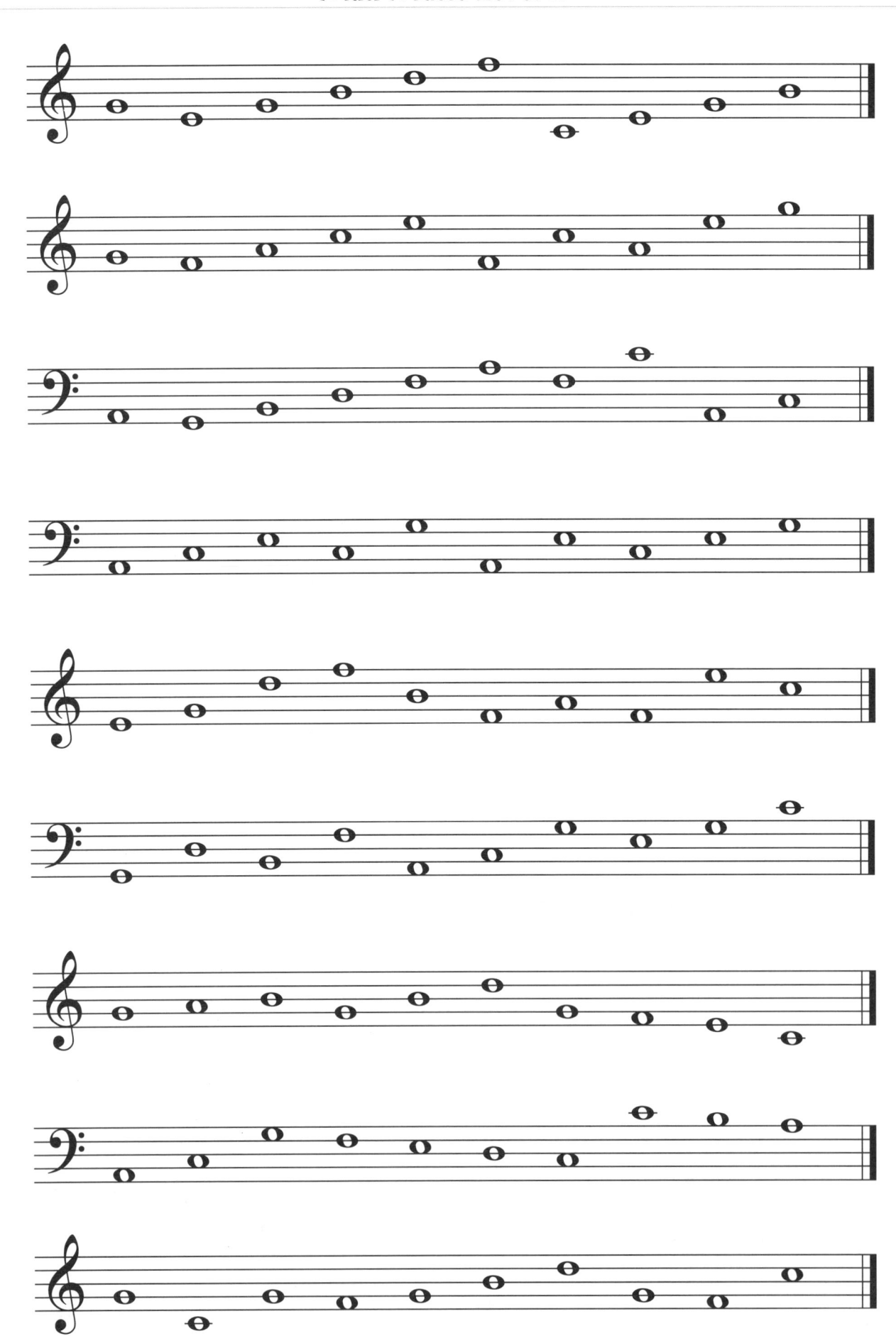

Charts and Games

Mad Music Level C

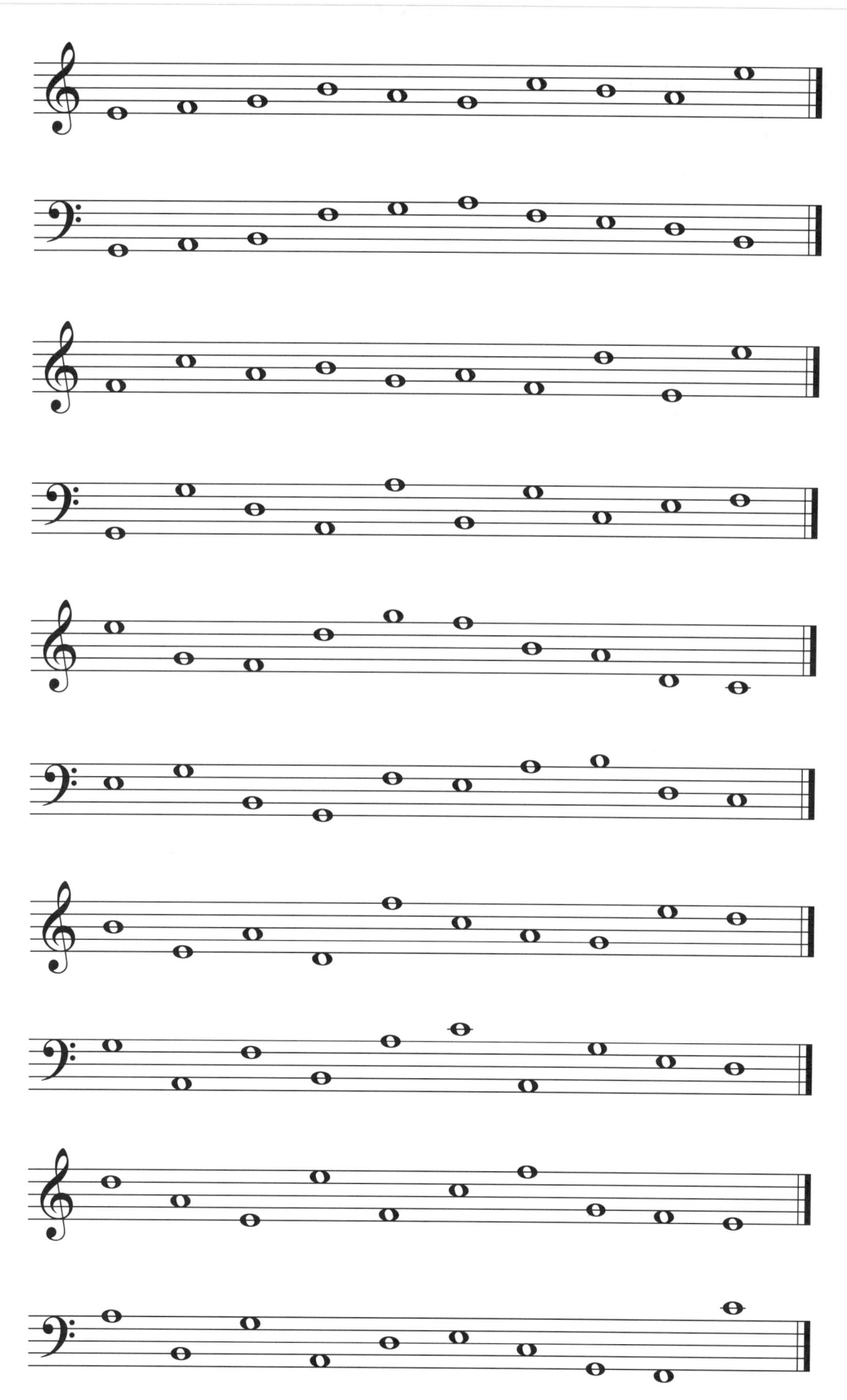

Sound Advice Level 1 — Charts and Games

Answer Keys

Lesson 1

1. Tempo Identification:

a) ☑ slow
   ☐ medium
   ☐ fast

b) ☐ slow
   ☐ medium
   ☑ fast

c) ☐ slow
   ☑ medium
   ☐ fast

2. Rhythmic Reading:

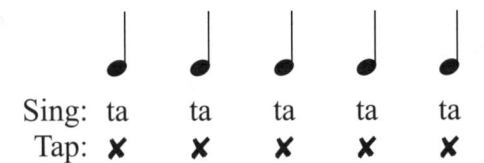

Sing: ta ta ta ta ta
Tap: ✗ ✗ ✗ ✗ ✗

3. Rhythmic Reading:

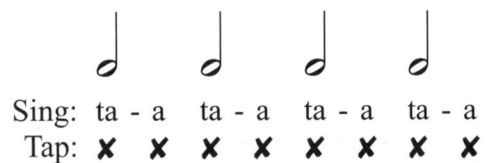

Sing: ta - a   ta - a   ta - a   ta - a
Tap: ✗   ✗   ✗   ✗   ✗   ✗   ✗   ✗

4. Rhythmic Identification:

5. Rhythmic Dictation:

---

122   Ear-Training Answer Key   Sound Advice Level 1

Ear-Training Answer Key

Lesson 2

1 Pitch Direction:

a) ☑ higher ☐ lower ☐ same

b) ☐ higher ☐ lower ☑ same

2 Pitch Direction:

a) ☑ up ☐ down ☐ repeat

b) ☐ up ☐ down ☑ repeat

c) ☐ up ☑ down ☐ repeat

3 Rhythmic Reading:

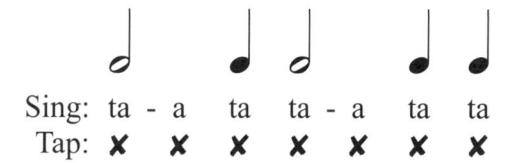

Sing: ta - a   ta   ta - a   ta   ta
Tap: ✗   ✗   ✗   ✗   ✗   ✗   ✗

4 Rhythmic Reading:

Sing: ta   ta   ta - a   ta - a   ta
Tap: ✗   ✗   ✗   ✗   ✗   ✗   ✗

5 Rhythmic Dictation:

Sound Advice Level 1   Ear-Training Answer Key   123

Ear-Training Answer Key

Lesson 3

Track 11

1 Rhythmic Reading:

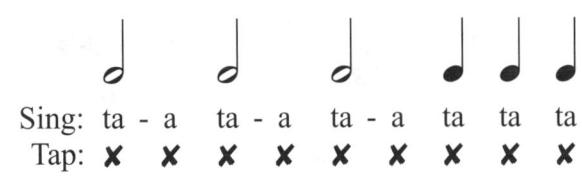

Sing: ta - a ta - a ta - a ta ta ta
Tap: ✗   ✗   ✗   ✗   ✗   ✗   ✗ ✗ ✗

Track 12

2 Rhythm Singback/Clapback:

Track 13

3 Rhythmic Dictation:

Track 14

4 Pitch Direction:

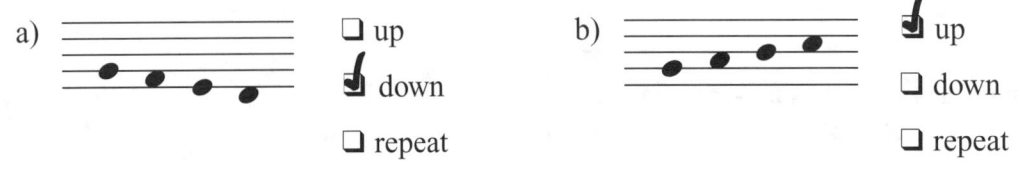

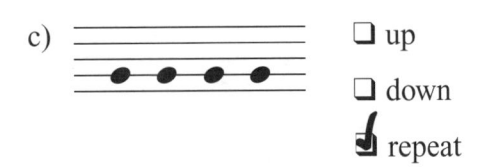

a) ☐ up
   ☑ down
   ☐ repeat

b) ☑ up
   ☐ down
   ☐ repeat

c) ☐ up
   ☐ down
   ☑ repeat

Track 15

5 Pitch Identification:

a) ☐   ☑   ☐

b) ☑   ☐   ☐

124 Ear-Training Answer Key Sound Advice Level 1

Ear-Training Answer Key

Lesson 4

1) Pitch Identification:

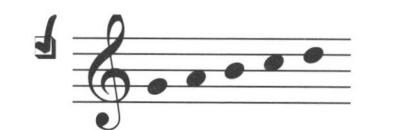

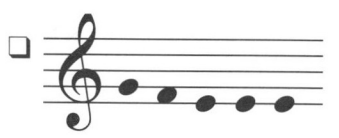

a) ☐ ☑ ☐

b) ☐ ☐ ☑

2) Rhythmic Identification:

a) ☐ ☑

b) ☑ ☐

3) Rhythmic Reading:

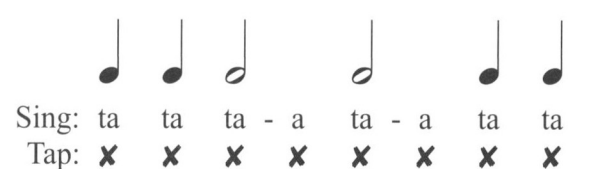

Sing: ta ta ta - a ta - a ta ta
Tap: ✗   ✗   ✗ ✗   ✗ ✗   ✗   ✗

4) Rhythm Singback/Clapback:

5) Rhythmic Dictation:

Ear-Training Answer Key

Lesson 5

1 Pitch Identification:

2 Rhythmic Identification:

3 Rhythmic Reading:

Sing: ta - a ta ta ta - a ta ta
Tap: ✗   ✗   ✗   ✗   ✗   ✗   ✗

4 Rhythm Singback/Clapback:

5 Rhythmic Dictation:

Ear-Training Answer Key

Lesson 6

1 Pitch Identification:

a)

b)

2 Rhythmic Reading:

Sing: ta - a ta ta - a ta ta ta ta
Tap: ✗   ✗   ✗   ✗   ✗ ✗ ✗ ✗

3 Rhythm Clapback:

Melody: Rhythm:

4 Rhythm Clapback:

Melody: Rhythm:

5 Rhythmic Dictation:

Ear-Training Answer Key

Lesson 7

1 Melodic Identification:

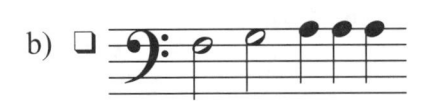

2 Rhythmic Reading:

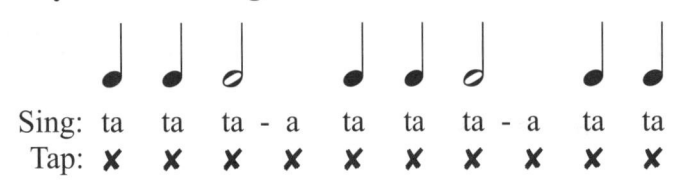

Sing: ta ta ta - a ta ta ta - a ta ta
Tap: ✗ ✗ ✗ ✗ ✗ ✗ ✗ ✗ ✗

3 Rhythmic Identification:

4 Rhythm Singback/Clapback:

5 Rhythmic Dictation:

Ear-Training Answer Key

Lesson 8

1 Rhythmic Reading: *(Track 36)*

Sing: ta ti ti ta ti ti ta ta ta
Tap: ✗ ✗ ✗ ✗ ✗ ✗ ✗ ✗ ✗

2 Rhythmic Reading: *(Track 37)*

Sing: ta ta ti ti ti ti ta - a ta - a ta
Tap: ✗ ✗ ✗ ✗ ✗ ✗ ✗ ✗ ✗

3 Rhythmic Identification: *(Track 38)*

a) ☐ ♩ ♫ ♩ ♫   ☑ ♩ ♫ ♩ ♫

b) ☑ ♫ ♫ ♩   ☐ ♫ ♫ ♩ ♫

4 Rhythmic Dictation: *(Track 39)*

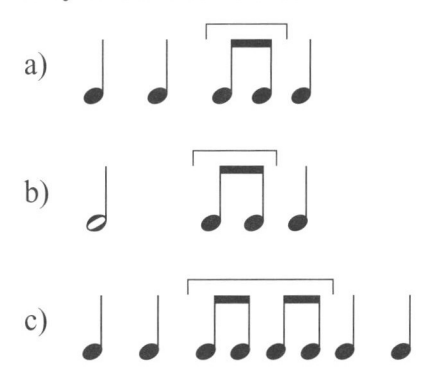

a) ♩ ♩ ♫

b) ♩ ♫

c) ♩ ♩ ♫ ♫ ♩

5 Rhythmic Dictation: *(Track 40)*

♩ ♫ ♩

Ear-Training Answer Key

Lesson 9

Track 41

1 Sight Singing:

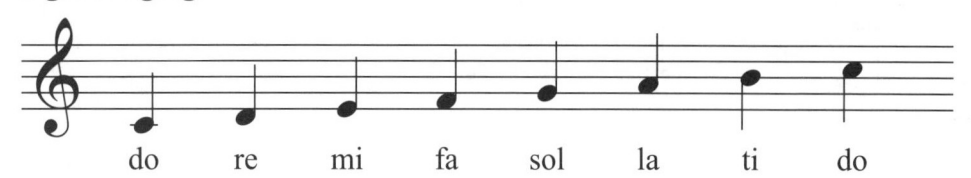

do re mi fa sol la ti do

Track 42

2 Error Detection:

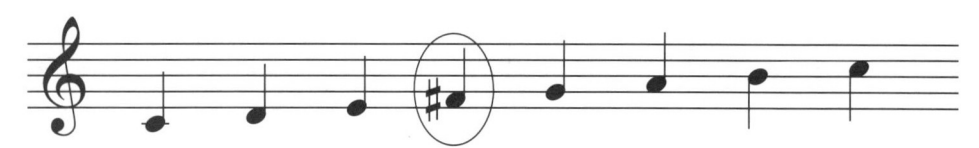

(the 4th note circled with a sharp)

Track 43

3 Melodic Identification:

a) ☑ (first option checked)

b) ☑ (first option checked)

Track 44

4 Sight Singing:

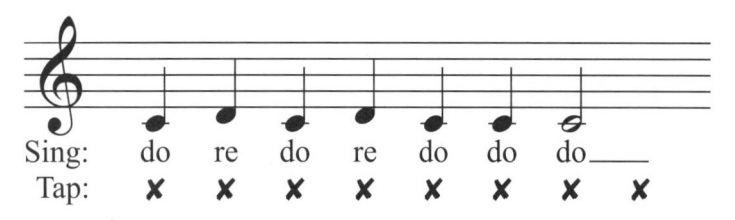

Sing: do re do re do do do___
Tap: ✗ ✗ ✗ ✗ ✗ ✗ ✗

Track 45

5 Melodic Dictation:

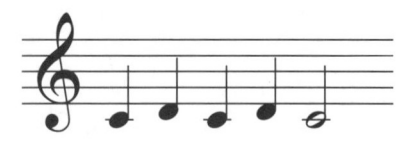

130   Ear-Training Answer Key   Sound Advice Level 1

Ear-Training Answer Key

Lesson 10

Track 46 — **1** Sight Singing:

do re mi fa sol la ti do ti la sol fa mi re do

Track 47 — **2** Error Detection:

Track 48 — **3** Melodic Identification:

Track 49 — **4** Sight Singing:

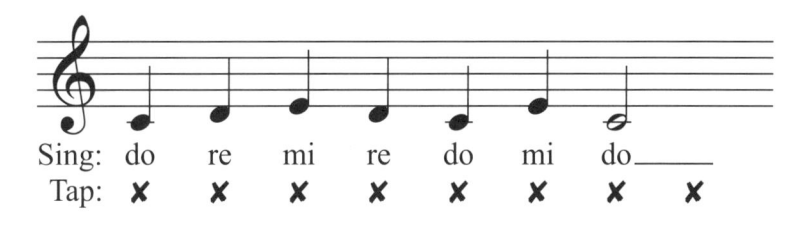

Sing: do re mi re do mi do___
Tap: ✗ ✗ ✗ ✗ ✗ ✗ ✗ ✗

Track 50 — **5** Melodic Dictation:

Track 51 — **6** Interval Identification:

a) 2nd   b) 3rd   c) 2nd   d) 2nd   e) 3rd

Sound Advice Level 1   Ear-Training Answer Key   131

Ear-Training Answer Key

Lesson 11

1. Rhythmic Identification:

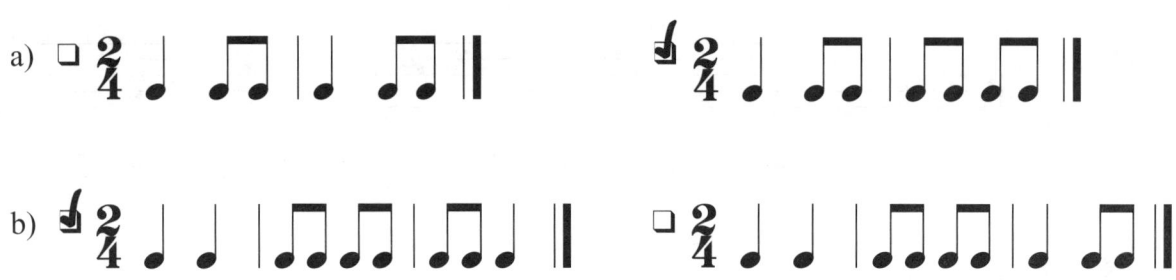

a) [2/4 notation] | [2/4 notation]

b) [2/4 notation] | [2/4 notation]

2. Rhythmic Reading:

Sing: ta ta ta ta ti ti ti ti ta ta
Tap: x x x x x x x x x x

3. Rhythmic Dictation:

[2/4 notation]

4. Sight Singing:

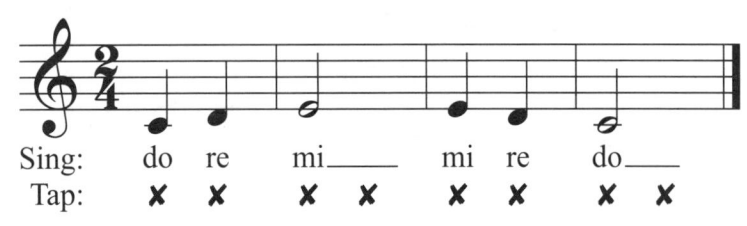

Sing: do re mi___ mi re do___
Tap: x x x x x x x x

5. Interval Identification:

a) 3rd   b) 3rd   c) 2nd   d) 3rd   e) 2nd

Ear-Training Answer Key

Lesson 12

1 Rhythmic Reading:

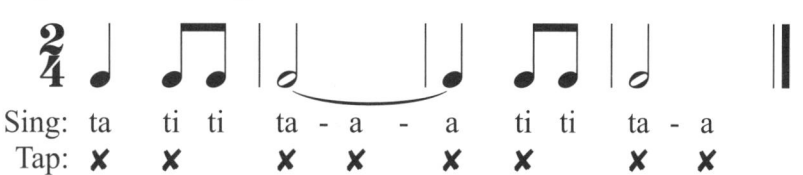

Sing: ta ti ti ta - a - a ti ti ta - a
Tap: ✗ ✗ ✗ ✗ ✗ ✗ ✗ ✗

2 Rhythmic Reading:

Sing: ta ti ti ta - m ti ta ti ti ta - m ti
Tap: ✗ ✗ ✗ ✗ ✗ ✗ ✗ ✗

3 Editing:

4 Rhythm Singback/Clapback:

5 Interval Identification:

a) 2nd   b) 3rd   c) 3rd   d) 2nd

Sound Advice Level 1   Ear-Training Answer Key   133

Ear-Training Answer Key

Lesson 13

1. Rhythmic Reading:

Sing: ta ti ti ta ti ti ti ti ta
Tap: x x x x x x x x x

2. Rhythmic Reading:

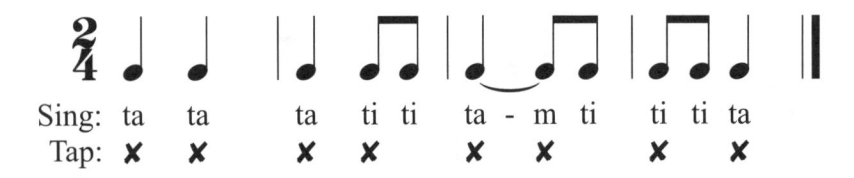

Sing: ta ta ta ti ti ta - m ti ti ti ta
Tap: x x x x x x x x x

3. Rhythm Clapback:

Melody:

Rhythm:

4. Sight Singing:

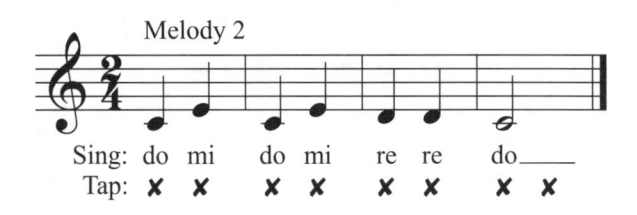

Melody 1

Sing: do re mi re do mi do___
Tap: x x x x x x x

Melody 2

Sing: do mi do mi re re do___
Tap: x x x x x x x x x

5. Melodic Identification:

6. Interval Identification:

a) maj 2   b) maj 3   c) maj 2   d) maj 2   e) maj 3

134   Ear-Training Answer Key   Sound Advice Level 1

Ear-Training Answer Key

Lesson 14

1. Sight Singing:

do re mi fa sol la ti do ti la sol fa mi re do

2. Sight Singing:

Sing: do re mi re do sol do___
Tap: x x x x x x x x

3. Interval Identification:

a) maj 2 b) P5 c) maj 3 d) maj 2 e) P5

4. Interval Identification:

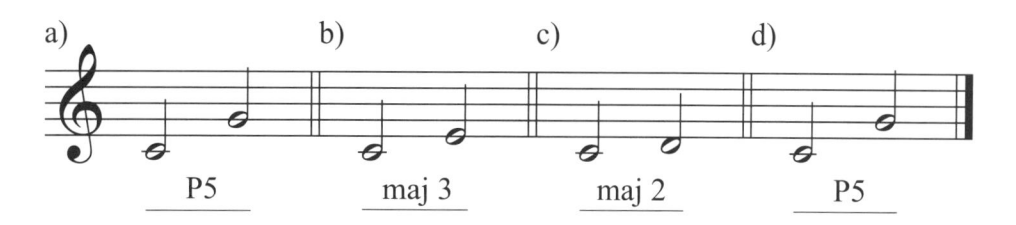

a) P5 b) maj 3 c) maj 2 d) P5

5. Editing:

Ear-Training Answer Key

Lesson 15

1. Rhythmic Reading:

Sing: ta ti ti ta ta - m ti ta ta ti ti ta - a - a
Tap: x x x x x x x x x x x x

2. Rhythm Clapback:

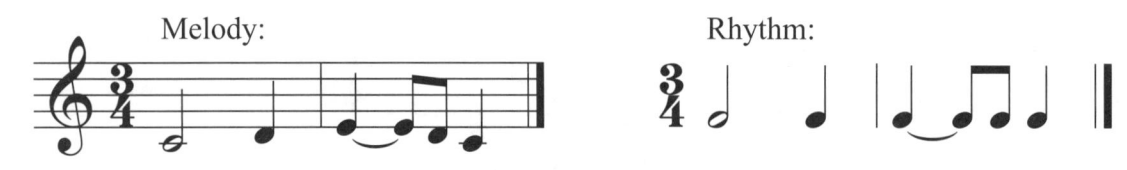

Melody:

Rhythm:

3. Interval Identification:

a) P5   b) maj 3   c) maj 2   d) P5   e) maj 3

4. Sight Singing:

Sing: do sol do mi___ re do___
Tap: x x x x x x x x x

5. Melody Singback/Playback:

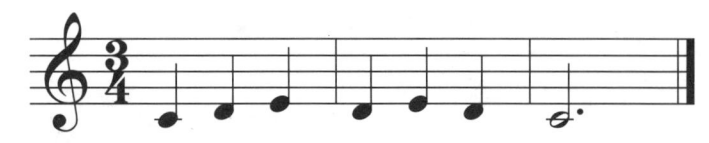

6. Meter Identification:

a) ☐ duple
   ☑ triple

b) ☑ duple
   ☐ triple

Ear-Training Answer Key

Lesson 16

1) Interval Identification:

a) maj 3   b) P5   c) maj 2   d) P4   e) maj 3

2) Sight Singing:

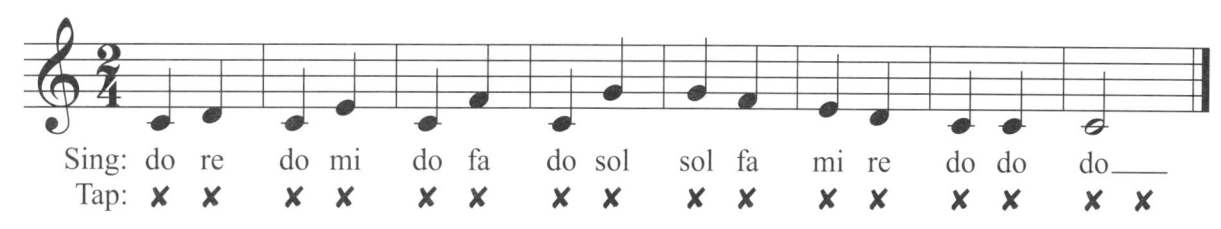

Sing: do re do mi do fa do sol sol fa mi re do do do___
Tap: x x x x x x x x x x x x x x x x

3) Melody Singback/Playback:

4) Rhythmic Dictation:

5) Melodic Dictation:

Sound Advice Level 1 — Ear-Training Answer Key

Ear-Training Answer Key

Lesson 17

1. Interval Identification:

a) P4   b) maj 2   c) P5   d) maj 3   e) P4

2. Melody Singback/Playback:

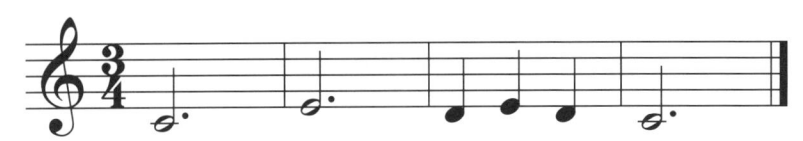

3. Rhythmic Dictation:

Melody: Rhythm:

4. Error Detection:

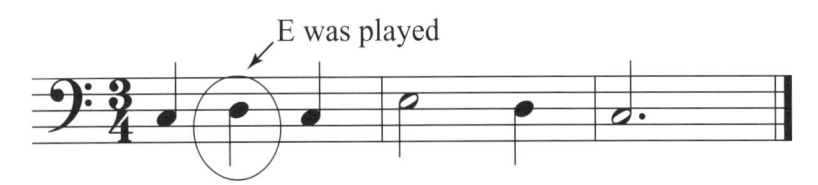

E was played

5. Editing:

Ear-Training Answer Key

Lesson 18

Track 89 — **1** Interval Identification:

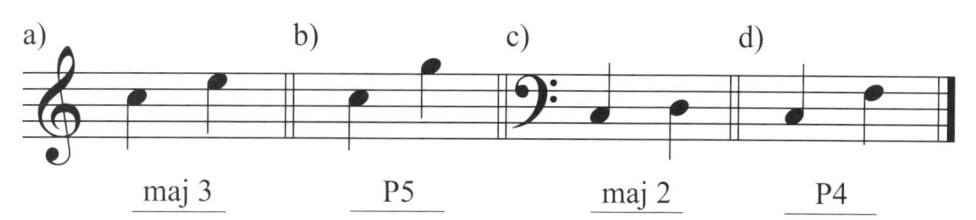

a) maj 3   b) P5   c) maj 2   d) P4

Track 90 — **2** Editing:

Track 91 — **3** Melodic Identification:

Track 92 — **4** Rhythm Clapback:

Melody: Rhythm:

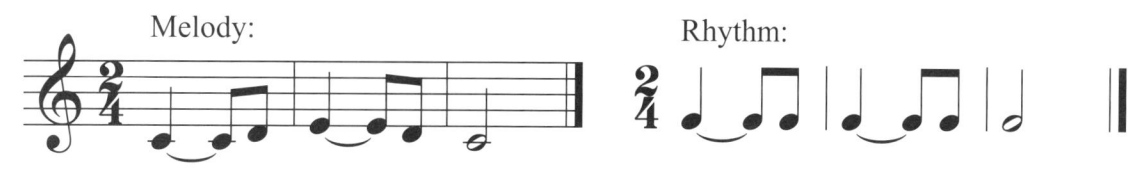

Track 93 — **5** Melodic Dictation:

Sound Advice Level 1 — Ear-Training Answer Key — 139

Ear-Training Answer Key

Lesson 19

1. Interval Identification:

a) min 2   b) maj 2   c) maj 2   d) min 2   e) maj 2

2. Rhythmic Reading:

Sing: ta - m ti ti ti   ta - m ti ti ti   ta ta   ta ti ti ta
Tap: x x x   x x x   x x x   x x x

3. Rhythmic Clapback:

Melody: / Rhythm:

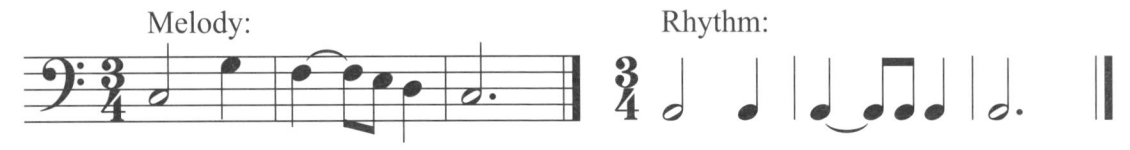

4. Sight Singing:

Sing: do— re mi fa sol— la ti— do ti— la sol— fa mi— re do—
Tap: x x x x x x x x x x x x x x x x

5. Melodic Dictation:

6. Error Detection:

D was played

140   Ear-Training Answer Key   Sound Advice Level 1

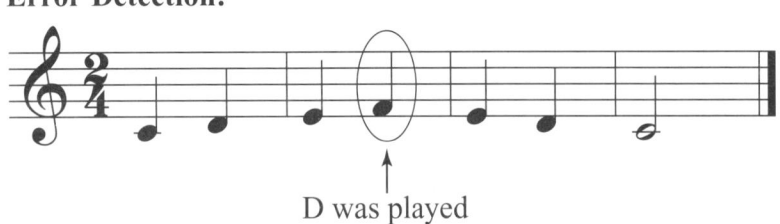

Ear-Training Answer Key

Lesson 20

1. Sight Singing:

Sing: do re mi fa sol la ti ti do
Tap: x x x x x x x x

2. Scale Identification:

Scale no. 1
☐ major
☑ not major

Scale no. 2
☑ major
☐ not major

Scale no. 3
☐ major
☑ not major

Scale no. 4
☑ major
☐ not major

3. Rhythmic Dictation:

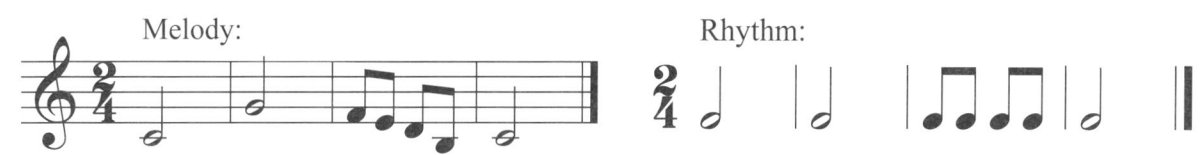

Melody: / Rhythm:

4. Melodic Dictation:

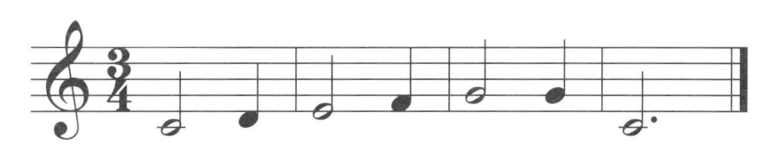

5. Meter Identification:

a) ☑ duple
   ☐ triple

b) ☐ duple
   ☑ triple

Sound Advice Level 1 — Ear-Training Answer Key

Ear-Training Answer Key

Lesson 21

1. Interval Identification:

a) P5   b) maj 2   c) P8   d) min 2   e) P4

2. Sight Singing:

Sing: do — do — ti la sol fa mi re do —
Tap: x x x x x x x x x x

3. Rhythm Clapback:

4. Rhythmic Dictation:

5. Melodic Dictation:

Ear-Training Answer Key

Lesson 22

1. Interval Identification:

a) maj 2   b) P8   c) maj 3   d) P4   e) min 2

2. Rhythmic Reading:

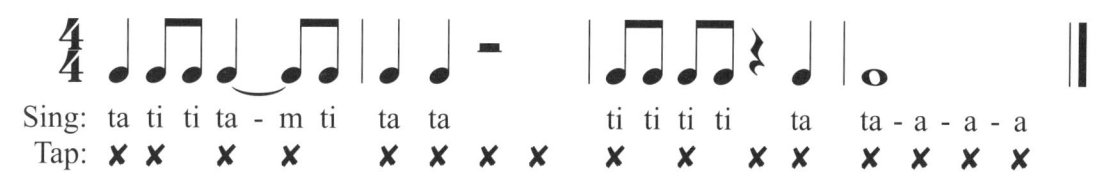

Sing: ta ti ti ta - m ti ta ta   ti ti ti ti ta ta-a-a-a

3. Rhythm Clapback:

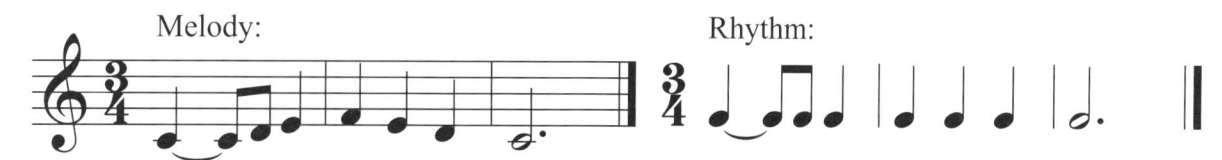

4. Sight Singing:

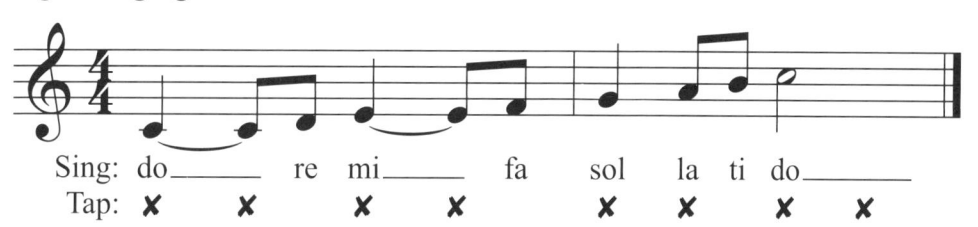

Sing: do __ re mi __ fa sol la ti do __

5. Melody Singback/Playback:

6. Error Detection:

E was played

Sound Advice Level 1 — Ear-Training Answer Key — 143

Ear-Training Answer Key

Lesson 23

1. Interval Identification:

a) P4   b) min 2   c) P5   d) maj 3   e) P8

2. Sight Singing:

Sing: do — re mi re — mi fa sol fa mi re do —
Tap: x x x x x x x x x x x x

3. Melodic Dictation:

4. Scale Identification:

Scale no. 1	Scale no. 2	Scale no. 3	Scale no. 4
☑ major	☐ major	☐ major	☑ major
☐ not major	☑ not major	☑ not major	☐ not major

5. Meter Identification:

a) ☐ duple   b) ☑ duple
b) ☑ triple   ☐ triple

Ear-Training Answer Key

Lesson 24

1. Interval Identification:

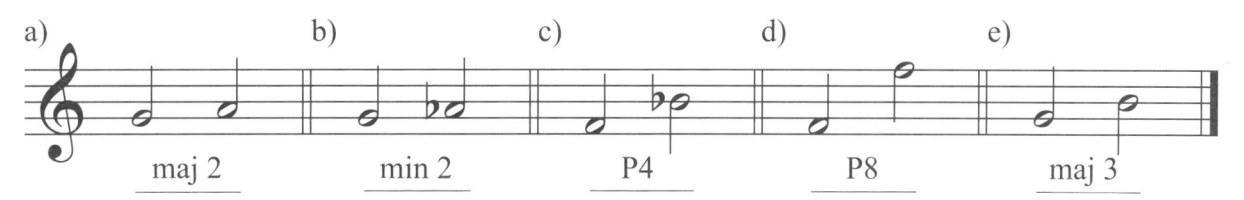

a) maj 2   b) min 2   c) P4   d) P8   e) maj 3

2. Sight Singing:

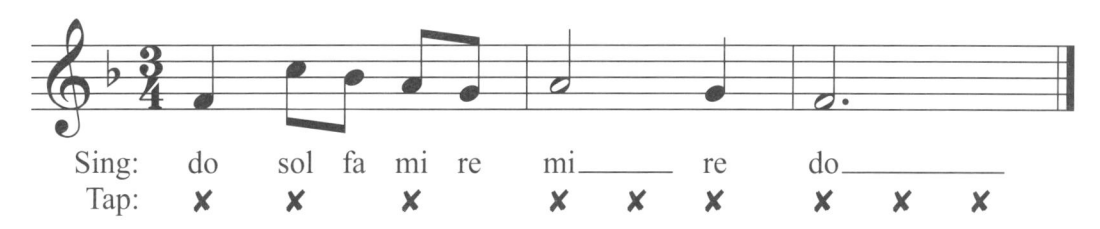

Sing: do sol fa mi re mi re do

3. Melody Singback/Playback:

4. Rhythmic Dictation:

5. Error Detection:

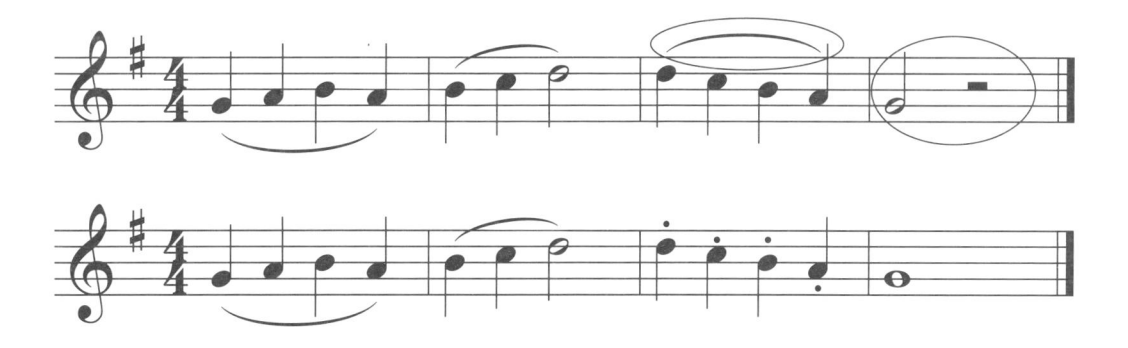

Sound Advice Level 1   Ear-Training Answer Key   145

Melody Master Answer Key

Set One

Check the appropriate box on p. 109.

Set Two

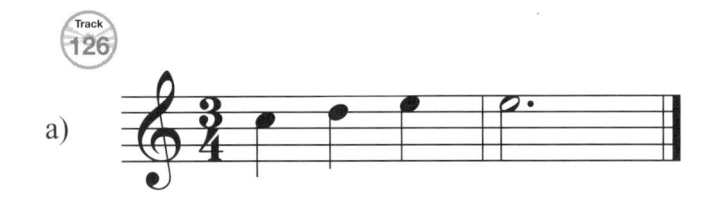

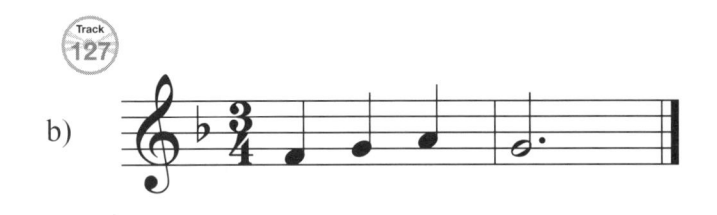

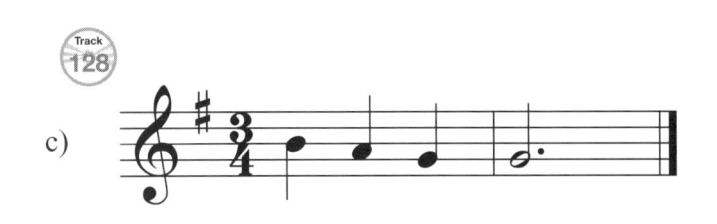

Check the appropriate box on p. 109.

Melody Master Answer Key

Set Three

a) [Track 136]

b) [Track 137]

c) [Track 138]

d) [Track 139]

e) [Track 140]

Set Four

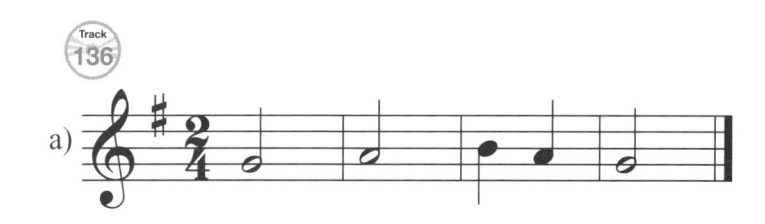

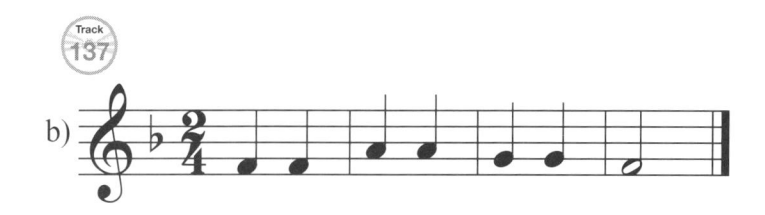

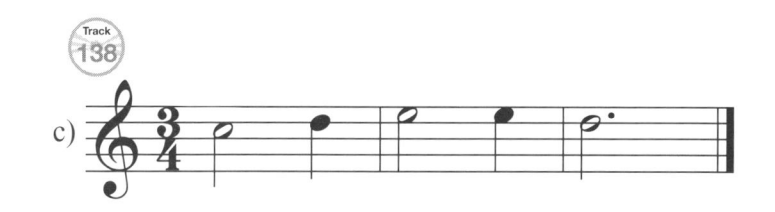

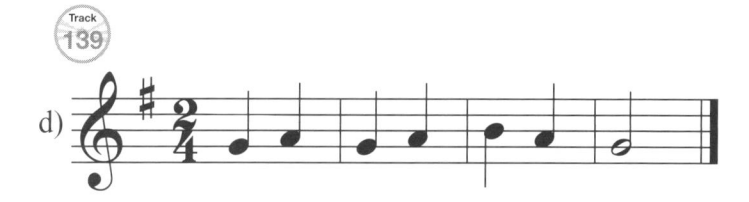

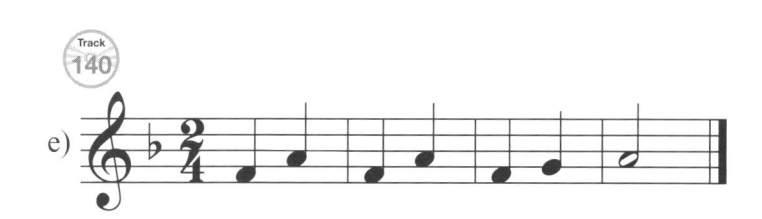

a) [Track 141]

b) [Track 142]

c) [Track 143]

d) [Track 144]

e) [Track 145]

Check the appropriate box on p. 109.

Check the appropriate box on p. 109.

Sound Advice Level 1   Melody Master Answer Key   147

Melody Master Answer Key

Set Five

a) (Track 146)

b) (Track 147)

c) (Track 148)

d) (Track 149)

e) (Track 150)

Check the appropriate box on p. 109.

Mad Music Answer Key

Level A

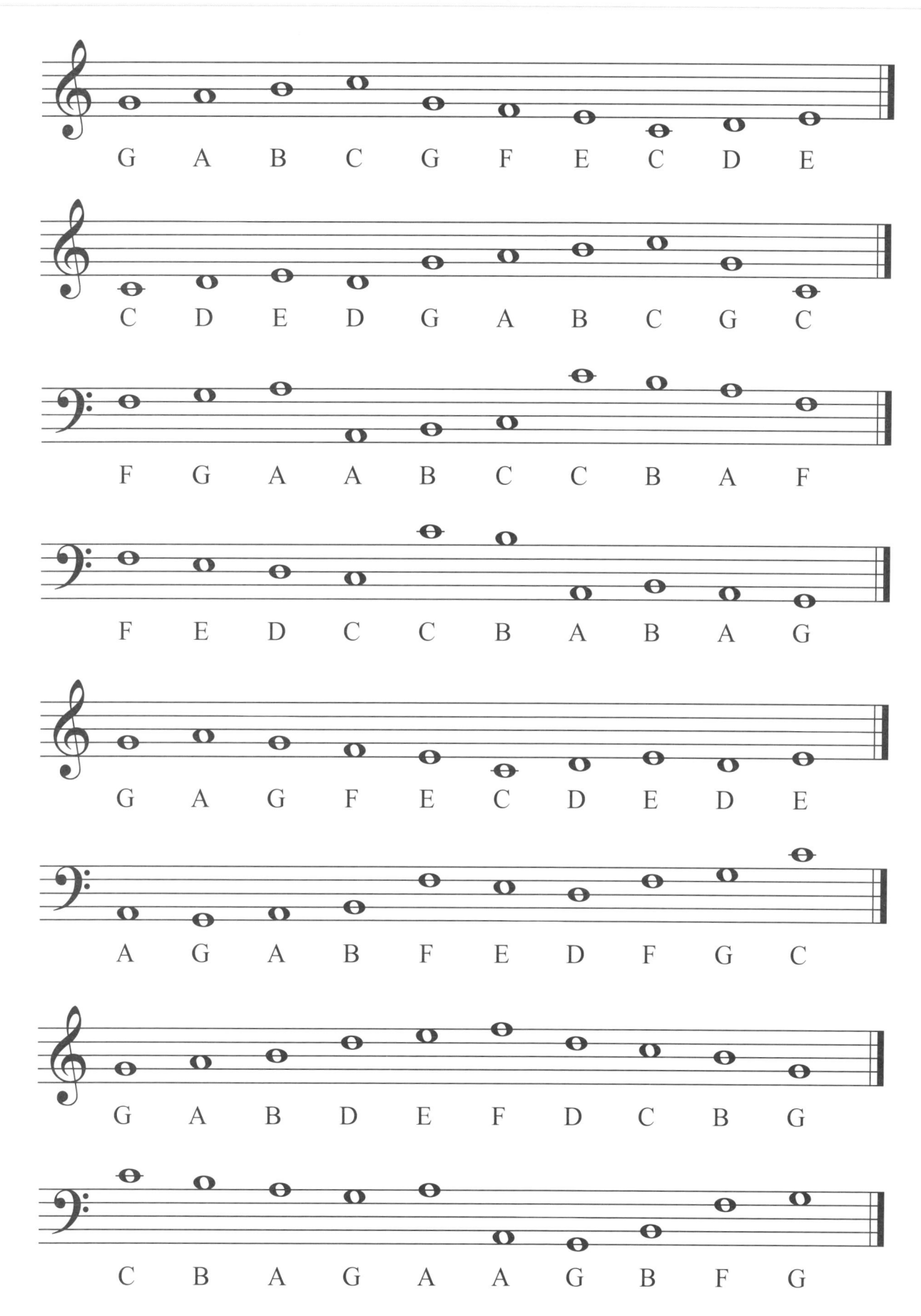

G A B C G F E C D E

C D E D G A B C G C

F G A A B C C B A F

F E D C C B A B A G

G A G F E C D E D E

A G A B F E D F G C

G A B D E F D C B G

C B A G A A G B F G

Sound Advice Level 1   Mad Music Answer Key   149

Mad Music Answer Key

Level B

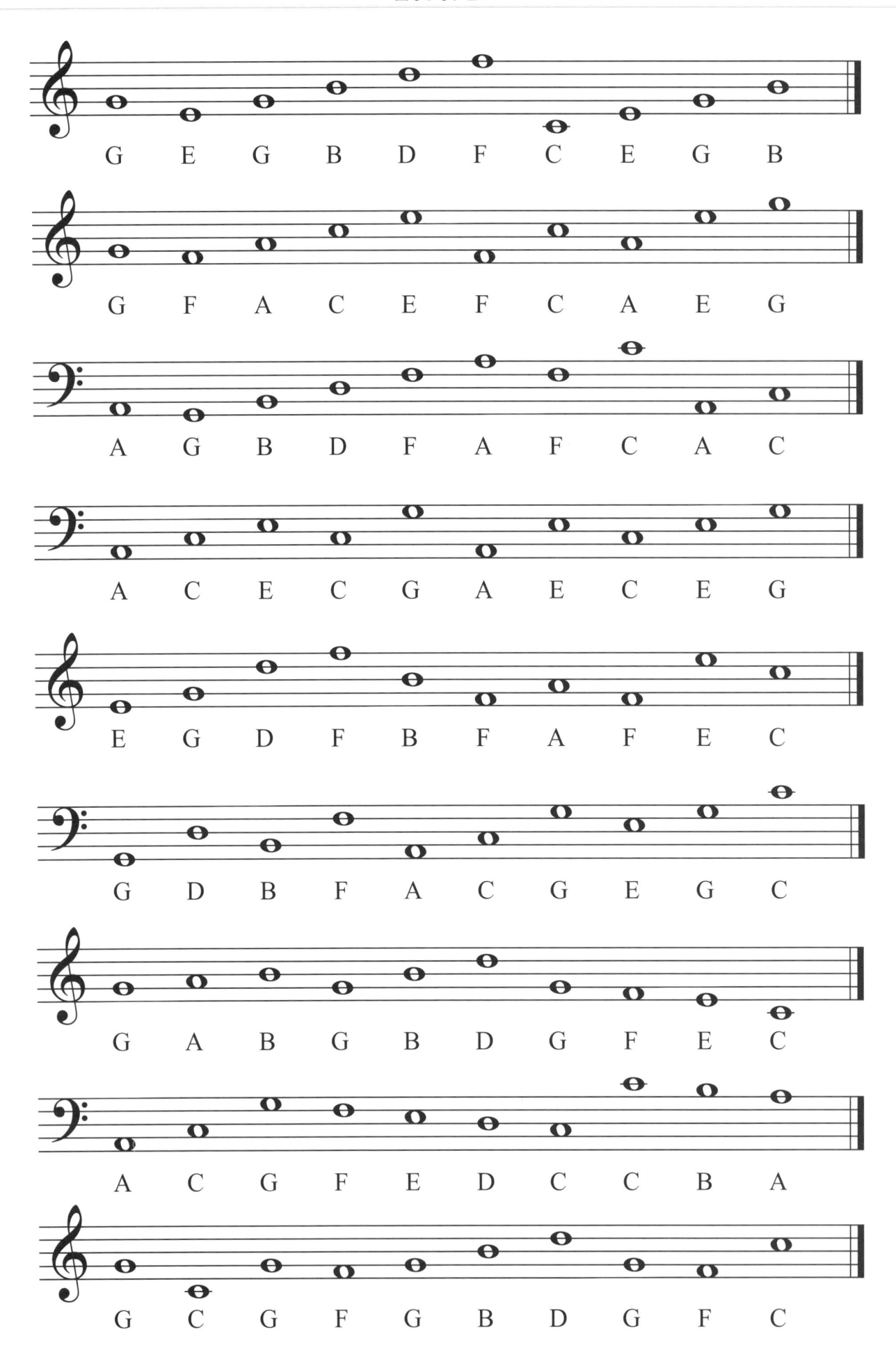

G E G B D F C E G B

G F A C E F C A E G

A G B D F A F C A C

A C E C G A E C E G

E G D F B F A F E C

G D B F A C G E G C

G A B G B D G F E C

A C G F E D C C B A

G C G F G B D G F C

Mad Music Answer Key

Level C

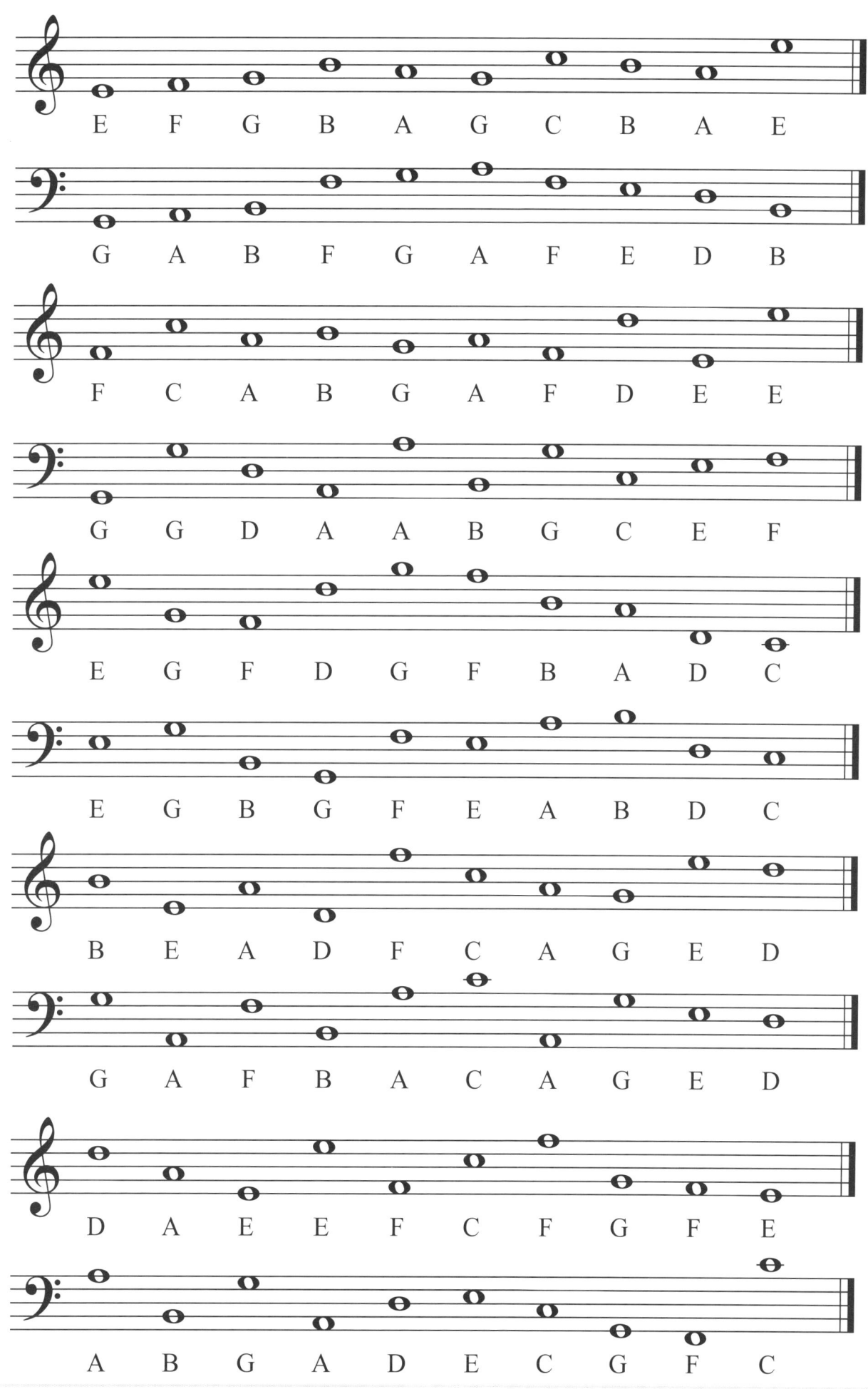

E F G B A G C B A E

G A B F G A F E D B

F C A B G A F D E E

G G D A A B G C E F

E G F D G F B A D C

E G B G F E A B D C

B E A D F C A G E D

G A F B A C A G E D

D A E E F C F G F E

A B G A D E C G F C

Sound Advice Level 1   Mad Music Answer Key   151

Appendix

Sight-Singing Syllable Systems

Movable Do

In the *movable do* system, do represents the tonic or first degree of the scale, regardless of key. Accidentals are accounted for by changing the syllables.

The syllables for the movable do system are:

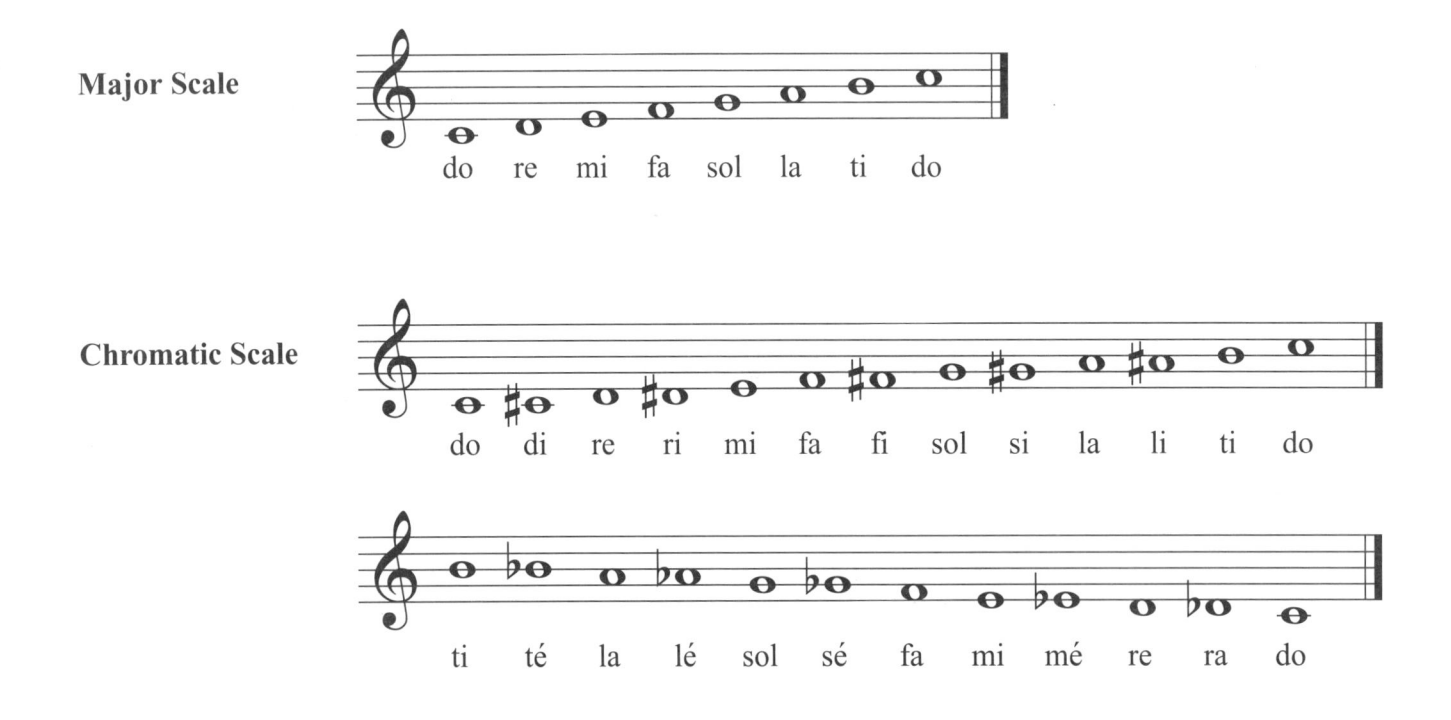

Major Scale

do re mi fa sol la ti do

Chromatic Scale

do di re ri mi fa fi sol si la li ti do

ti té la lé sol sé fa mi mé re ra do

Numbers

In this system, numbers ($\hat{1}, \hat{2}, \hat{3}$, etc.) are used instead of syllables (do, re, mi, etc.). A caret (^) above a number identifies that number as a scale degree. The tonic or first degree of the scale is always $\hat{1}$, regardless of key. There is no numerical change for chromatic notes on the same degree of the scale.

Fixed Do

In the *fixed do* system, the syllables coincide with letter names of the notes, regardless of key. For example, C is always do, F is always fa, and so on. The syllables used in the fixed do system are the same as those shown above for the chromatic scale.